in our changing culture that has grown less friendly to followers of Jesus."

—**Derwin Gray**, pastor
of Transformation Church
and author of *The HD Leader*

"This book will prove to be most helpful to young Christians who are confused about their values and how to interface with a culturally tumultuous world. It will provide a biblical rationale for many moderately conservative believers to engage in new ways of practicing good faith."

—**Jim Henderson**, Jim Henderson
Presents

"Deep inside every Christian is a desire to make an impact on the world around them. But too often there is a large divide between such desire and the actual impact. Believers can feel powerless in a culture that is pushing hard against what they stand for. The church has believed lies regarding our involvement in culture, and we have withdrawn into our Christian communities, taking our influence with us. *Good Faith* is a much-needed book for this hour because it slams into that powerless feeling and calls us not to retreat but to engage. Gabe Lyons and David Kinnaman call Christians to use their faith to make society a better place, and more importantly, they equip us to walk in courage and hope. "

—**Banning Liebscher**, founding pastor,
Jesus Culture

"Most of us know Christians who are strong on convictions, but you would not want them to represent you as a fellow believer to the broader culture. On the other hand, there are many Christians who are so strong on civility you have no idea what they believe. In *Good Faith* we have practical tools for living out our faith in a rapidly changing culture."

—**Mark A. Yarhouse**, PsyD,
Rosemarie S. Hughes Endowed Chair
and professor of psychology
at Regent University

"This book is an act of leadership that Christians need to follow. Because it gets right to the guts of the botched conversation between churched and unchurched people, *Good Faith* is a must-read for pastors, students, and everyday Christians who want to have better conversations about faith."

—**Dr. Todd Hunter**, founding bishop of
Churches for the Sake of Others
and founding pastor
of Holy Trinity Anglican Church

"How do we live out our faith in America today in a way that is both true to God's Word and culturally relevant? In a way that turns people to God rather than away from him? This is a tough question that Willie and I grapple with daily and one that all Christians should be asking themselves. God calls us to be salt and light to this world. He asks us to live in it but not be of it. Boldly and with love, *Good Faith* lays out how we just might do that. It's an important book for all believers to read."

—**Korie Robertson**, *Duck Dynasty*

"Jesus's first followers were on fire with a world-changing mission, and they transformed their culture. Gabe Lyons and David Kinnaman give clarity to the challenges Christians face while inspiring us to recognize the power we have to rekindle a flame that will transform our world."

Richard Stearns, president, *World
Vision US* and author of *The Hole
in Our Gospel*

"When the issues of our day threaten to divide the Church, we must lean in with wisdom and truth while loving with abandon and grace. For any generation, living in this tension is no easy task. Gabe and David are leading the way for the Church and help us faithfully navigate the new terrain."

Jennie Allen, founder and visionary,
IF:Gathering, and author
of *Restless* and *Anything*

GOOD
FAITH

BEING A CHRISTIAN
WHEN SOCIETY THINKS
YOU'RE IRRELEVANT
AND EXTREME

DAVID KINNAMAN
AND GABE LYONS

BakerBooks

a division of Baker Publishing Group
Grand Rapids, Michigan

© 2016 by David Kinnaman and Gabe Lyons

Published by Baker Books
a division of Baker Publishing Group
P.O. Box 6287, Grand Rapids, MI 49516-6287
www.bakerbooks.com

Printed in the United States of America

Library of Congress Cataloging-in-Publication Data

ISBN 978-0-8010-1317-1 (cloth)
ISBN 978-0-8010-1918-0 (paper)

Unless otherwise indicated, Scripture quotations are from the *Holy Bible*, New Living Translation, copyright © 1996, 2004, 2007 by Tyndale House Foundation. Used by permission of Tyndale House Publishers, Inc., Carol Stream, Illinois 60188. All rights reserved.

Scripture quotations labeled NIV are from the Holy Bible, New International Version®. NIV®. Copyright © 1973, 1978, 1984, 2011 by Biblica, Inc.™ Used by permission of Zondervan. All rights reserved worldwide. www.zondervan.com

Scripture quotations labeled NKJV are from the New King James Version. Copyright © 1982 by Thomas Nelson, Inc. Used by permission. All rights reserved.

Authors are represented by Christopher Ferebee, Attorney and Literary Agent, www.christopherferebee.com.

16   17   18   19   20   21   22   7   6   5   4   3   2   1

We dedicate this book to our children

Emily, Annika, and Zachary Kinnaman

and

Kennedy, Pierce, and Cade Lyons

with the prayer that it serves you well as a small guide
to following Jesus in the days ahead

CONTENTS

Part III
THE CHURCH AND OUR FUTURE

PART I

UNDERSTANDING OUR TIMES

1

BAD FAITH, GOOD FAITH

Extremist. In our part of the world these days, this word is about as aggressive an insult as you can throw down in polite company, instantly associating the recipient with rifle-brandishing ISIS militants, Paris bombers, or Boko Haram kidnappers.

In some people's eyes, if you are a devoted Christian today, this label now describes you.

Do you believe Jesus is the only way to heaven? Extremist. Prayed for someone you don't know? Extremist. Believe marriage is meant to be between one man and one woman? Extremist. Would you give up a good-paying job to do mission work? Extremist. Do you believe Christians have a responsibility to talk about Jesus with nonbelievers, even with strangers? Extremist.[1]

Something—a backlash against religion's worst sins, a political climate that wants to stamp out religion in public life, the popular rise of atheism, amplified access to polarizing points of view, *something*—is making it increasingly difficult to practice faith in our society.

For many people of faith, it's becoming harder to live their convictions outside of their religious communities. It feels as though forces are pushing religion to the margins. In fact, to millions of people, faith is irrelevant or even bad news. "Religion poisons everything" declares the subtitle of one of the bestselling books of our new century.[2]

Many Christians—and believers in other faith traditions as well—are feeling overwhelmed, sidelined, and misunderstood. They feel typecast as bigoted, judgmental, and hypocritical. The sense for many believers is that society is hostile to faith in general and to Christianity in particular.

This isn't just a feeling. When one-third of college-aged adults want nothing to do with religion, and 59 percent of Christian young adults drop out of church at some point in their twenties, it's the new reality on the ground. Culturally, it seems like a landslide victory for the other side . . . whoever that is.

This book aims to address the questions, *What does the future hold for people of faith when people perceive Christians as irrelevant and extreme?*

In what ways can faith be a force for good in society?

How can people of faith contribute to a world that, more and more, believes religion is bad?

Faithful Is Not Extreme

Whether or not we like the cultural trends, we need to get a handle on reality and chart a way forward.

People of every religious tradition—and secularists too—make claims about the nature of reality and how humans ought to live within it. Most people believe their own religion's (or nonreligion's) appraisal of reality is true. And not just "true for me"—true for human beings everywhere. Eight out of ten practicing Christians, for example, agree the Bible contains moral truths that are true for all people without exception.[3]

This bothers some people. They believe religion should be consigned to the realm of the private, to family home and house of worship—no exceptions.[4] They claim "real" life happens in laboratories and the marketplace and boardrooms and city halls. They are convinced that spirituality and other fluffy, intangible stuff matter only peripherally to "real" life. And their views are gaining currency in our culture.

- More than two out of five Americans believe that, when it comes to what happens in the country today, "people of faith" (42 percent) and "religion" (46 percent) are part of the problem, rejecting the idea that religious individuals could be part of the solution.[5]

- More than eight out of ten practicing Christians say religious freedom has become more restricted because some groups are actively trying to move society away from traditional Christian values.

- Further, the public's perceptions of the clergy have changed. Fifty years ago clergy members were commonly viewed as among the most important leaders of our society. They were trusted sources of wisdom across a wide spectrum of issues. But the public's respect for pastors, priests, and other faith leaders has significantly declined. Today only one-fifth of US adults strongly believe that clergy are a credible source of wisdom and insight when it comes to the most important issues of our day.

Or consider how attitudes have changed when it comes to public expressions of religious commitment. As Western culture continues to become more secular, many of the everyday acts of devotion practiced by people of faith—Christians, Jews, Muslims, and many others—are increasingly considered inappropriate by ever wider swaths of the growing nonreligious population.

In other words, more people are skeptical of hard lines and strong convictions, preferring a watered-down tolerance over a hard-won peace. A new generation is reflexively suspicious of anything that smacks of piety. For these folks, a life lived with religious conviction is not just countercultural or counterintuitive but dangerous, even damaging. In their view, if you raise your children to embrace the same convictions, you are beyond extreme; you may be criminal.[6]

People of good faith, however, contend that every thought, word, and deed are meant to be weighed on the scale of faith, that faith should be the primary lens through which life is perceived, that science, commerce, business, politics, and every other sphere of human endeavor are at their best when approached from a distinctly theological point of view.

But what does it mean for Christians today?

To put it broadly, a theological approach insists that God is at the center of life, not on the periphery. Faith has implications for all of life, not just for the hour or two a week when like-minded believers gather to worship and pray.

These believers, like us, contend that faith, when it's done right, is *good*. It is good not only for the faithful but for nonbelievers as well. Lived well and practiced consistently, good faith may be the best hope for our neighbors and society as a whole.

The aim of this book is to make a case for good faith. Christianity has managed to survive and thrive as a minority religion countless times throughout history—and does so in many places around the world today. So we hope you'll gain confidence that holding tight to biblical conviction is not only worthwhile and critical but also absolutely doable. Despite the faults we Christians bring to it, Christianity practiced well helps people thrive and communities flourish. Together, we want to discover how Christians can do good for *and* with the people around us—even when doing so may, at first, be an unwelcome advance.

Good Faith will prepare you to be smart and courageous and to live faithfully in a changing culture that is no longer particularly friendly to faith.

At best, diverse, pluralistic cultures, like that of North America today, are indifferent to people of faith; they accept only the most tepid, inoffensive forms of religious expression. At worst, they are actively hostile toward religious practices and beliefs (one recent op-ed called them "superstitious rituals" and "comically outlandish claims"[7]). This book touches on many topics that crowd the intersection of faith with the wider culture: sex and sexuality, politics, race, religion and public life, morals and virtues, and many more.

When it comes to good faith, everything must be on the table.

Difficult Conversations

Of course it was in an elevator—where you can't escape an awkward conversation. I was visiting a posh part of London, and a fellow hotel guest asked, "What kind of event is happening here?"

I explained, "It's a conference for church leaders. Christians are here from all over the world to listen and learn from one another."

Smugly, he replied, "I have an idea for your Christian conference: why not hold it in a less expensive place than London and give the money you save to the poor?"

"Well, there are many reasons for being here. The conference is hosted by a church that's located in this neighborhood, and they've got loads of volunteers and places to meet at no cost. So it's actually less expensive for the conference to be hosted here than in many other places."

Not satisfied, the middle-aged skeptic and his companion edged out the door to the fourth floor as he muttered, "Whatever. It makes no sense to me!"

I called to the closing doors, "I'd be happy to talk more if you want . . ."

Don't you just hate it when people don't want to hear you out?

The next morning at the hotel's breakfast buffet, the same man sat just a table away. Knowing I was taking a risk, I said, "Good morning," as friendly as I could.

He seemed startled, and then slightly annoyed, to see me again. He grunted a hello, then picked up where he'd left off the previous evening: "Did you come up with an answer to my question? Why are you guys here wasting money?"

Man, this guy is relentless, I thought. "As I was trying to explain yesterday, there are lots of good reasons, like . . ."

I couldn't get the words out before he cut me off. "There is only *one* good answer. Don't waste your money. Your priorities are screwed up!" Pointedly, he turned his full attention to his eggs, beans, tomatoes, and bacon.

The discussion was over. In a few minutes, he gathered his things and left.

* * *

It's hard to have a good conversation these days, especially about faith. Even when two people pretty much agree, honest interaction seems elusive. But being friends across differences is hard, and cultivating good conversations is the rocky, uphill climb that leads there. Good conversations demand active listening, mental and emotional engagement, openness to the possibility that we're wrong, and empathy to see the situation from the other person's point of view.

Now throw in some genuine differences of opinion—profound gaps in religious viewpoint or worldview—and a good conversation is further out of reach. Try to talk about things like gay marriage—or anything remotely controversial—with someone you disagree with and the temperature rises a few degrees. At times, it feels as if the other person is speaking a different language, or he's deliberately misjudging your point of view, or you're both assuming the worst about each other. What might have been a good conversation—where both people feel heard, understood, and respected—degenerates into defensiveness, name-calling, accusations, bitterness, and even hatred. Good conversations, our best hope for peace in conflicted relationships, are on the endangered species list.

Our research shows that having meaningful conversations is increasingly difficult for many of us. This is true not only on an individual level but also society-wide. Why is a good conversation so difficult to find these days?

First, it's not enough to be nice. When it comes to conversations about beliefs, morals, and faith, Christians have often emphasized the importance of being winsome and engaging. The thinking—driven by the right impulse—is that if Christians could be *reeeeeally* nice about things, then others would at least respect the people behind the beliefs.

We'll make the argument, however, that it's no longer sufficient for Christians to be winsome. Being winsome is not bad. It's good. But aiming for niceness as our ultimate goal can give us a false sense of making a difference in people's lives. And as you will see in the research we conducted for *Good Faith*, many of the basic ideas Christians believe are perceived as irrelevant and extreme. Nice doesn't overcome the perception that Christians are crazy.

More and more people think the Christian community is completely out of step with the times. No matter how kind or friendly believers are in presenting their beliefs, it's not likely to make much of a difference. Many folks have their minds made up that Christian ideas are outlandish. These people might listen for entertainment's sake, but Christians have little chance of breaking through to real understanding.

Now, this is not an excuse to be less kind. Far from it. Rather, it's an invitation for Christians to rethink our manner of being "in the world but not of it." We hope this book is a map for the path forward.

An uncomfortably large segment of Christians would rather agree with people around them than experience even the mildest conflict. According to this perspective, it's never right to criticize people or their decisions and lifestyles.[8] By adopting this value without much reflection, many Christians have stuffed their convictions. When Christians cram their deepest beliefs so far down, there's little hope those beliefs could ever affect real conversations. We acknowledge that our times are complex and relationships are complicated. These facts don't mean, however, that we should not try to see and communicate about reality more clearly. It *is* hard to agree on what's best, but taking ourselves out of the conversation to avoid conflict doesn't help anyone.

Second, the gaps between people groups seem to be growing. Even if they've been there all along, the divides have widened on social media and twenty-four-hour cable news. There are gaping fissures between rich and poor, between races, between genders, between faith groups, between political parties, and so on. Generation, gender, socioeconomics, ethnicity, faith, and politics massively divide us. Just look at the furor ignited in Indiana over religious liberty legislation and in Kentucky over marriage licenses. Or consider the protests in Ferguson and Baltimore that escalated into violence. Even *inside* the Christian community there are acute divides between various "tribes."

The bottom line is that many of our social structures—the institutions and rhythms that keep us whole and healthy as a society and as individuals—are unwinding.[9]

Third, social media, for all the remarkable benefits of digital tools like Facebook, Twitter, Snapchat, and Instagram, can make connecting across these gaps more difficult, not less. In spite of the truly wonderful gifts of the digital revolution, social media at its worst can magnify our differences, making it even harder to have conversations that matter. For one thing, it can make it more difficult to see other people for who they really are. For another, it helps us find the tiny cliques of people who are already convinced of the crazy things we believe. Social media makes it far too easy to self-select voices that always affirm and never challenge our assumptions and sacred cows. Plus, many of our sanest thinkers and leaders are choosing to stay out of the fray altogether. They've clued in that the most strident and extreme voices are liked, shared, and retweeted—not the most reasonable ones.

How do you think social media has changed our capacity for healthy, effective, *good* conversations about our differences?

According to Barna research, most people believe these digital tools have made meaningful dialogue and deep connection more difficult. In fact, 61 percent of adults say they believe social media has made people less social, less capable of deep friendships and strong connections. Furthermore, Americans are twice as likely today to say they are lonely compared to ten years ago.

Social media doesn't always make us more social.

How can we have conversations that matter on important issues between people and between groups of people? How can we believe with conviction and courage while reknitting social and spiritual bonds?

Our intention for *Good Faith* is to take a factual, realistic look at the challenges of living faithfully in our new cultural reality and then to help the community of faith respond effectively—both individually and collectively.

An Unfamiliar Landscape

Your guides are two guys who have worked together before, on a project called *unChristian*. When it released in 2007, that book presented the North American church with an "outsider's view" of itself and challenged individual Christians and church communities to seriously consider the critiques offered by young nonbelievers. It has been nearly a decade since then, and countless local churches have accepted the challenge to take a hard, humble look at how they practice and communicate their faith. With more awareness of the attitudes of young people, they are more intelligent about how to engage topics such as politics, sexuality, social issues, and pop culture and how to describe what following Jesus requires.

We decided to work together again on *Good Faith* because we see extraordinary opportunities for Christians to lead our culture today in a fresh and compelling way. There are plenty of challenges too, of course. And we are duty-bound to give you the brutal reality—but with hope. In the face of a tough cultural context, we have a deep-rooted hope that God's people can understand the times and know how to engage well (see 1 Chronicles 12:32).

To map the terrain for this project, Barna Group interviewed thousands of US adults and more than one thousand faith leaders, including Protestant pastors and Catholic priests as well as Jewish, Muslim, Mormon, and other clergy. The goal was to get an accurate lay of the cultural landscape, particularly of the places where communities of faith feel friction with their surrounding culture—and vice versa.

Good Faith walks through the findings of Barna's studies and other research and examines the implications for how we live and practice our faith now and in the future. All this new work has excavated two perceptions about Christians that are gaining cultural ground.

We are *irrelevant* and *extreme*.

Irrelevance is primarily about the rising tide of apathy toward religion overall and Christianity specifically. In our last book together, we talked a great deal about the hostility of younger non-Christians toward Christianity—and admitted there was some truth to their perceptions. Yet an even more significant challenge may be that growing numbers of adults, and especially younger adults, have no inkling that Christianity matters and could matter to them. Furthermore, they have little appreciation for how Christians generate good in the world.

The perception of extremism is the second major obstacle for Christians today. Many very bad things are legitimately called extremism and should be prevented by society. Yet some religious beliefs and practices are considered extremist not because they are violent but just because they're different. How should Christians navigate these choppy seas to engage with people who don't see things the same way?

The research for *Good Faith* leaves little room for doubt that the world is changing around us, making it harder for people to live faithful lives. There are doubts about who to believe and whether the Bible can be trusted, and these fault lines are sometimes pulling Christians and churches apart. However, the hard work of writing this book has generated in us a sense of awe and love for the Christians, churches, and faith organizations we work with. All of us together as Christ-followers have an amazing opportunity to shape the next decade of Christian witness in the world. As authors and leaders, husbands and fathers, we know it is a profound honor to be on mission with Jesus and his followers in this crazy, complex culture!

Still, given the increasing tension many Christians are experiencing, the two of us felt compelled to come together again. This book is meant to help our Christian sisters and brothers find footing on unfamiliar terrain. To accomplish this, we pulled from every available resource at our disposal:

brand-new social research, interviews and conversations with a broad range of leaders with diverse views, our own hard-won lessons, including stories of our personal shortcomings. We examined the habits of good faith Christians so we can learn from them and grow in our own lives. Just as in *unChristian*, we resist name-calling or finger-pointing. What good would that do?

This book offers a framework for thinking and living, including practical suggestions for how to respond to our changing society. Our prayer is that, despite the stiff headwinds we face, this project will fill you with renewed hope and purpose.

We believe that when people commit to a Jesus-shaped way of life, they create a counterculture for the common good—living their lives not for themselves but for the benefit of others to the glory of God. If we do this, we can reshape the imagination of our culture so that the gospel can renew hearts and minds in the generations to come.

Let's take a deeper look at the two negative perceptions facing Christians today.

2

IRRELEVANT

Board games are not my thing. I enjoy many other activities: watching movies, making conversation, eating great food, reading compelling books, painting, and woodworking. But not playing board games. On rare occasion, in a sheer act of will and of love for my family, I will sit down and play.

Other members of the Kinnaman family feel differently. My brother, Matt, and my son, Zack, *love* board games. They visit websites with game rankings. They put plastic sleeves on the cards of their card-based games to protect them from the greasy hands of non-gamers. They know secrets about dice combinations I can't even imagine. They are game fanatics.

Zack and I took a cross-country flight last year to visit Matt, Kate, and their kids in Virginia. It was February, and snow and ice had turned my brother's place into a cozy little igloo. So out came the beloved board games. By my count, Matt taught us *six* new board games during that stretch of wintery nights.

The first two were great. I hung in there, learning the rules of play—even enjoying myself.

At 11 p.m. on the second night, after the toddlers were asleep, Matt pulled out *another* new game: Roll for the Galaxy. I am not kidding: there were *hundreds* of multicolored dice, all with strange and unfamiliar icons.

Matt launched into an explanation of the game's intricate rules. Zack focused on his uncle's instruction with a disciple's zeal and intensity. My son had ears to hear and eyes to see the "game gospel" proclaimed by his rabbi, Uncle Matt.

Pan to my face: eyelids half-mast, ears tuning out. I was *so sleepy.* For all I knew, we may as well have been talking about *actual* space exploration to visit the planet Xenon. I had no idea what the different colored dice meant, much less the alien icons. Matt tried to explain the nuances of the game in the simplest possible terms, but to me his voice had never sounded so soothing. The only parts of my brain that were working were the synapses searching for an excuse that wouldn't hurt the feelings (too much) of my dear brother and his young acolyte.

To a lot of people in our culture, this is what Christianity feels like.

Background Noise

Irrelevance happens when your interests and someone else's don't overlap—like trying to share with someone the joy of playing your favorite game when to them board games are joyless, soul-sucking instruments of torture. (That's a joke, Matt and Zack.) The other person may admire your passion but cannot relate to it.

For increasing millions of people in the wider culture, Christianity feels like a long list of rules that matter *to someone else.* Some try to hang in there out of a sense of duty or obligation. They might make a sincere effort to participate in church, maybe because it's important to people they care about. But Christianity just doesn't stick.

They never roll for the galaxy, much less search out their salvation. They can't understand how or why faith relates to them, so they look for an excuse to leave the table.

Through our research, we have sorted out clear ways to distinguish those who see faith as background noise from those actively engaged in the game. We call the latter group "practicing Christians," people who say their Christian faith is very important in their lives and attend church at least once a month. These are folks for whom Christianity is a way of life, not just a cultural identifier. Three out of ten Americans are practicing Christians.

For many millions of people who might be considered "legacy Christians," however, Christianity is background noise that can safely be ignored. They have the muscle memory of being a Christian but exercise little faith in their lives today. They used to be active or grew up as a Christian, but now the tenets and practices of the faith are just part of the landscape, not guiding lights for their priorities and lifestyle.

We could count this group of people—legacy or nominal Christians—as the largest faith group in America today. Three out of four US adults have some Christian background, but about three in five American Christians are mostly inactive in their faith.

Using our earlier analogy, you might think of legacy Christians as people who learned the rules of the game years ago, but at some point the rules, and participating in the competition itself, became almost entirely irrelevant. When we interview them about why they don't prioritize their faith or participate in faith-related activities, legacy Christians tell us they are just too busy or they find God elsewhere—in nature or art, for instance. To them, church is boring. Christianity has faded into the background. It's a way of life that matters to somebody else.

How Irrelevant? Let Us Count the Ways

Most legacy Christians think Jesus-followers who prioritize faith are irrelevant and maybe annoying but also largely benign. But others, usually the religiously unaffiliated, think Christianity is bad for society. We are not seen as people of good faith.

Let's try to see ourselves from their perspective.

Perception: Christian Leaders Aren't Credible Guides for Life

As we touched on in chapter 1, perceptions about the trustworthiness of Christian ministers have plunged over the past half century. For example, how reliable a source of information and counsel do US adults believe pastors and priests are on a variety of issues? On the obviously "spiritual" issues, these leaders do fairly well: one-third of adults say Christian leaders are *very* reliable when it comes to offering wisdom about God's will for human beings and about how the church can help people live according to God's will. Another one-third of adults say ministers are *somewhat* reliable as sources of counsel in these areas.

But on issues closer to the ground, pastors are less integral. Only one out of six US adults say Christian leaders are very reliable guides for how Christianity should inform our political and justice systems. And only 25 percent of adults say ministers are very reliable in helping people live out their convictions privately and in public.

On the whole, pastors and priests are well liked—two-thirds of Americans say their presence is a benefit to a community—but their insights are not considered relevant to living real life. You might say Christian leaders are viewed like a smiling greeter at Walmart: they might point you in the right direction, but after that you're on your own.

This perception is a huge problem. For so long these leaders' influence kept the moral and spiritual dimensions of human life on our culture's radar. Who will replace them as trustworthy guides for living?

Perception: Faith-Driven Organizations Are Irrelevant to a Charitable Society

Millions of adults are oblivious to how charity happens. Our research shows that up to half of Americans believe a majority of the charitable work in the nation—including providing food, clothing, shelter, counseling, and disaster relief, for example—would still happen if there were *no* religious people or organizations to do that work.[1] Among those who claim no religion, nearly three out of five believe most charitable work would continue without Christians. Shockingly, 17 percent of practicing Christians believe the same, reflecting a lack of confidence in Christian contributions to society. Although their view is far from reality, perceptions matter.

Some people are now calling for the end of tax-free benefits to religious nonprofit organizations because they believe the government shouldn't subsidize these kinds of groups. This line of reasoning (1) fails to see the tangible, far-reaching good churches and faith-based organizations do in and for our shared society and (2) equates tax exemption with government support. Of course no organization should be released from financial accountability, legal oversight, and good governance. But the perception of religion's irrelevance to the common good, taken to its logical conclusion, is that all religious organizations should contribute money to the government based on their revenues.

We think it's this dire: if we don't adequately address questions of good faith, the future of charity is at risk. If tax-free status were revoked, thousands of churches and other faith-based nonprofit organizations would cease to operate, removing their impact on the common good. This would be a calamity.

Donations to religious causes and groups make up the largest single share of national charitable giving, one-third of all money donated to nonprofit organizations.[2] Financial generosity is one of the places good faith has the most traction. A massive amount of work for the common good gets done precisely because of religious people and organizations. And because of the historical patterns of Christianity in the United States, this work is largely done thanks to Christians.

I (Gabe) was part of a meeting with thirty other faith leaders in 2009 hosted by the White House's faith-based division. After President Obama was elected, Joshua Dubois, the director of Faith-Based and Neighborhood Partnerships, was quick to convene leaders to consider how the government and Christian organizations could collaborate to accomplish more good together. On the table were projects such as reforming the prison system, hunger relief, combating sex trafficking, and fighting extreme poverty around the world.

After an inspiring few hours hearing about all the great work Christian-led organizations were doing, I pulled one of the White House aides to the side and asked, "Are you pulling in other religious groups for these conversations too?"

His reply was hushed but telling: "Yes, but it doesn't have the same leverage. It's Protestant evangelicals and Catholics who are doing the most work in these areas."

Many non-Christian organizations contribute to the common good, and overall giving to churches has fallen off over the past fifty years, so let's not break our arms patting ourselves on the back.[3] But if Christians' resources and passion to do good in the world were suddenly to evaporate, great harm would come to our society and its most vulnerable people.

Yet a majority of non-Christians believe the social good Christians do in Christ's name is negligible. Irrelevant even.

Perception: Christianity Is Irrelevant to the "Real Stuff" of Life and Culture

Most people think Jesus was a pretty good guy, but they don't believe his teaching has made much of an impact on modern society. Large proportions of the population, even Christians, believe our faith has had little or no impact on art, culture, personal well-being, politics, community cohesion, charitable behavior, and provision of community services. Among non-Christians, the perceived line dividing the Christian faith and societal impact is even more distinct.[4]

Furthermore, many people dramatically underestimate the number of practicing Christians in sectors that power our economy and create a healthy society. Public education is just one example. According to Barna estimates, two out of every five public school teachers and administrators in the United States are practicing Christians. It would be folly to say that, simply because Christians are present, public schools don't have challenges. But millions of Christ-followers bring their good faith to public education, working for lower pay than in many other industries because teaching kids, for many of them, is a vocation—part of their calling. As one Christian educator told us, "Even if there is no official prayer in schools, I am there praying every day." And this is just one sector of society; practicing Christians do good work and meaningfully contribute across a wide spectrum of industries.

For good faith Christians, work is an expression of worship.

Perception: People Can Live a "Good Life" without Christianity

For many people, life seems pretty good without faith. They can play the "game of life" without using the Christian rule book and still experience what feels like "winning." Christians also believe this is true—to a certain extent. Jesus offers abundant and eternal life to those who follow him, but it's certainly possible to live a decent and productive life without being a Christian. We see this all the time. Mahatma Gandhi, to take an obvious example, was not a Christian, yet he clearly lived a life that even today, nearly seventy years after his death, impacts the world for the better.

The fact that people can live meaningful, fulfilling lives without Jesus does not invalidate the claims of Christianity. Christ is the rightful ruler of this world and is redeeming its inhabitants from sin, evil, and death. But we should acknowledge that the "good life" feels attainable to many people—75 percent of US adults agree "a person can live a pretty good and decent life without being a Christian"—and this keeps them feeling like Christianity is a board game that isn't worth learning.

Part of the problem is that too many in the Christian community have bought into unbiblical notions about what it means to live a "good life," so it doesn't look, to outsiders, like we're doing anything special. Rather than living as a counter-cultural community that bears witness to the coming kingdom of God, many of us go with the cultural flow, thoughtlessly consuming the products, ideas, and aspirations streamed for us in an unending deluge of retweets and Facebook likes. It's so hard, in this screen age, to keep our attention focused on anything for very long—much less a way of life introduced to Middle Eastern peasants two thousand years ago. Talk about irrelevant! Christianity's rootedness in past events and future hope seems, to many, out of step with the *now* orientation of the hyperlinked life.

Perception: Many of Christianity's Good Ideas Feel Like Normal Life

Many people have no idea that some of the essential institutions of our society emerged from the Christian worldview. And they have forgotten the good faith Christians throughout the centuries who profoundly and positively shaped the institutions we enjoy today: schools and universities, hospitals, labor unions, public libraries, voting rights for women and ethnic minorities, endowments for the arts and sciences, and on and on. While they may have begun as Christian impulses to bless the world, most of these institutions are now divorced from the religious urges that brought them to life. For instance, the Puritan founders of Harvard, Yale, and other Ivy League schools were committed Christians, but few people today think of those venerable institutions as "faith-based."

Even arenas that were once the faith community's exclusive domain have been de-faithed, so to speak.

There are now companies that offer mission and service trips without any faith connections.

Nonreligious nonprofits solicit donations to feed the hungry, clothe the naked, and heal the sick.

Mainstream magazines preach the benefit of digital breaks, a spinoff of the biblical idea of Sabbath.

Personal meditation retreats without religious trappings are all the rage.

Business leaders talk of community flourishing, social good, and human well-being.

Politicians shepherd their flocks toward transcendent goals.

Celebrities testify to the physical and spiritual benefits of fasting.

Life coaches help people find their purpose and calling.

There's nothing inherently wrong with any of this. In fact, these de-faithed cultural movements point, in some way, to the enduring *relevance* of Christianity. Christian ideas have merit in the broader culture. Yet the next question practically asks itself: Now that the wider culture has co-opted many of Christianity's good ideas, what more does Christianity have to contribute?

Do we really want people to sit down and learn the rules of this ancient faith when their "normal" seems just fine without it?

Yes, we do.

From Irrelevance to Good Faith

Being a Christ-follower means proclaiming him as Lord and sharing the good news of his coming kingdom with those who don't know him. But we may as well acknowledge that, according to society's shifting values, living faithfully under the lordship of Christ *is* increasingly irrelevant. Our culture's underlying moral and ethical standard has become "do what you want as long as you don't hurt anybody." By that standard, "proclaim Jesus as Lord and live under his rule and reign" is . . . well, irrelevant.

However, we maintain that, by proclaiming and living under Christ's reign, we can work for the common good *in ways that are relevant* to the majority culture. (To be clear, just because an increasingly secular and narcissistic society thinks the gospel is irrelevant doesn't mean that it *is* irrelevant. In fact, sharing the gospel is one of the most relevant things we can do!)

Part of the vision for this book is that together we can gain a better understanding of how to live and act in good faith today, to follow Paul's admonition in Romans 12:2: "Don't copy the behavior and customs of this world, but let God transform you into a new person by changing the way you think. Then you will learn to know God's will for you, which is *good* and pleasing and perfect" (emphasis added).

We will do this, at various points, by meeting people who are living out a Jesus-shaped way of life, sometimes in the unlikeliest of places. People like Anne.

We both met Anne Snyder more than half a dozen years ago. She was just three years out of a Christian college in the Midwest and now worked in Washington, DC. Having spent her first professional gigs toggling between academia and journalism, she'd just landed a dream job. "David Brooks hired me to be his editor and research assistant a few months ago," Anne told David. "You know, the *New York Times* columnist?"

Right.

"That's so cool. What's that like?"

"So far it means I'm a sounding board, someone to read his early drafts of columns, or to track down stats, or to offer story ideas. It's both meaningful and fun. And I can't believe I am getting to do this so soon out of school."

Anne is exceedingly intelligent and articulate, so it wasn't a surprise to us. But it *was* surprising that this young, professionally green evangelical Christian was working so closely with an influential public voice—prominent journalist, thought leader, Yale and Duke lecturer, and non-Christian.

Fast-forward to mid-2015. The same David Brooks releases a critically acclaimed book, *The Road to Character*. Having heard great things about it, I pick up a copy in the Denver airport. I read the first few chapters and am blown away by the strength of the book's writing and arguments. *Hey*, I wonder to myself, *wouldn't it be cool if Anne got a mention in the book?* I skim the end of the acknowledgments, expecting her name to show up in the long list of people authors scramble to thank right before their books go to print.

Bummer. Not there.

Wait.

I turn the page to the *beginning* of the acknowledgments, where Brooks writes:

Anne C. Snyder was there when this book was born and walked with me through the first three years of its writing. This was first conceived as a book about cognition and decision making. Under Anne's influence, it became a book about morality and inner life. She led dozens of discussions about the material, assigned me reading from her own bank of knowledge, challenged the superficiality of my thinking in memo after memo and transformed the project. While I was never able to match the lyricism of her prose, or the sensitivity of her observations, I have certainly stolen many of her ideas and admired the gracious and morally rigorous way she lives her life. If there are any important points in this book, they probably come from Anne.[5]

Wow! Anne Snyder. I know her! I thought.

And then the story beneath the story began to dawn on me: Anne's vibrant faith—and her God-given brilliance, uncompromising work ethic, and extensive reading list—had influenced Mr. Brooks in a profound, and relevant, way.

Her faithful presence made a difference.[6] In good faith, Anne made Christianity a little more relevant to one person, who happens to write bestselling books and a regular column for the *New York Times.*

3

EXTREME

Most people grow out of an adolescent obsession with anything nasty or gnarly, but in some of us there remains a sick fascination with the extreme gross-out. It's hard to look away, and part of us doesn't want to. My woodshop-teaching Grandpa Kinnaman used to "fix" blood blisters under his fingernails by using a power drill to—warning to the squeamish—bore a hole in his nail to relieve the pressure. Watching his self-surgery was horrible but also mesmerizing. You couldn't *not* look.

Human beings are different from other creatures in our attraction to extremes: diets, coupons, hobbies, sports, home remodeling, hoarding—you name it.

Think about the massive popularity of TV shows and You-Tube videos about anything "extreme." Extreme makeovers. Extreme home makeovers. Extreme weight loss. X Games (the *X* is short for "extreme"). *American Ninja Warrior. Shark Week.*

Eating exotic foods on a dare (call it *schadenfreude*, but be honest: it's hard to avert your eyes when someone is choking down fried grasshoppers or sautéed animal gonads).

The Wrong Kind of Extreme

If the past decade and a half has taught Americans anything, it's that religious extremism is a real thing. Bombarded by images of terrorism, gun violence, perpetual religious wars, and unthinkable atrocities, we are justifiably wary of people who use their faith as an excuse to do violence and incite terror.

However, perhaps out of fear instilled by 9/11 and an obsession with making ourselves "safe" in a world that is clearly not safe, our society too often counts religious conviction and public observance in the same column with religious extremism. Countercultural faithfulness is conflated with radicalism.

Is it extremism when people live according to what they believe to be true about the world? We can debate whether their worldview gives a true accounting of reality, but even if it does not, the fact that they believe and act differently than the mainstream does not necessarily make them extreme. And yet there is a clear move in US society toward this very idea.

Most people believe being religiously extreme is a threat to society. Three-quarters of all Americans—and nine out of ten Americans with no faith affiliation—agree. But what actions and beliefs, exactly, come to mind when people think about religious extremism?

We asked Americans eighteen and older their views on more than a dozen ways people of faith might express or observe the convictions of their religion.[1] We found, as you might expect, that using religion to justify violence against others is almost universally condemned as extremist: more than nine out of ten adults agree doing so is "very" or at least "somewhat" extreme.

But we also discovered that, nowadays, you don't have to hijack a plane, blow up a subway train, or cut off somebody's head to be considered an extremist. The perceptions of extremism hit close to home for most Christians, as you'll see in the table on the next page. Many historic Christian beliefs and practices are considered to be extreme by large proportions of Americans—especially among non-Christians. For example, two out of five adults believe it is extremist to try to convert others to their faith; 60 percent of all adults in America and 83 percent of atheists and agnostics believe evangelism—one of the central actions of Christian conviction—is extremist. A slim majority says that holding the belief that same-sex relationships are morally wrong is extremist. Two out of five adults believe it's extreme to quit a good-paying job to pursue mission work in another country.

Even at the bottom of the list, many essential Christian practices are now perceived to be extremist. While not majority opinions, millions of adults contend that behaviors such as donating money to religious causes, reading the Bible silently in public, and even attending church or volunteering are examples of religious extremism.

What most concerns people about extremism is the *public* expression of religion—when beliefs and practices enter the public square. For the most part, people think you can do whatever you want on Sunday mornings, in your churches, just so long as matters of faith don't spill out into society.

Religious Activities Considered Extreme by US Adults

Here are some things that people do for religious reasons—that is, actions or at-titudes motivated by their faith or beliefs. Please indicate whether you think these actions are very extreme, somewhat extreme, not too extreme, or not at all extreme.

% "very" + "somewhat" extreme

	% US Adults	% Evan-gelicals[a]	% Practicing Christians	% Other Faiths	% Atheists, Agnostics, Unaffiliated (No Faith)
Use religion to justify violence against others	93	93	92	96	94
Refuse to serve someone because the customer's lifestyle conflicts with their beliefs	83	53	68	88	89
Demonstrate outside an organization they consider immoral	64	25	49	71	73
Attempt to convert others to their faith	60	10	29	63	83
Believe that sexual relationships between people of the same sex are morally wrong	52	5	25	55	75
Protest government policies that conflict with their religion	51	15	33	58	60
Quit a good-paying job to pursue mission work in another country	42	13	25	36	47
Wear special clothes or a head covering for religious observance	31	28	28	26	32
Adhere to special dietary restrictions for religious reasons	29	20	22	20	34
Wait until marriage to have sex	24	5	11	20	34
Read the Koran (or Qu'ran) silently in a public place	18	21	23	16	14
Regularly donate money to their religious community (tithing)	18	0	12	15	27
Read the Bible silently in a public place	11	0	11	10	13
Attend church, synagogue, or temple on a weekly basis	7	0	7	5	11
Volunteer to help people in need	6	0	8	2	8

[a] For Barna's full definitions of "evangelical" and "practicing Christians" see the Glossary.

Source: Barna OmniPoll, August 2015, *N* = 1,000

Beyond the specific religious activities we assessed, broadly speaking, the perception of extremism is firmly entrenched among the nation's non-Christians. Forty-five percent of atheists, agnostics, and religiously unaffiliated in America agree with the statement "Christianity is extremist."

That's just shy of half.

Almost as troubling is the fact that only 14 percent of these "nones" (a term used to describe the religiously unaffiliated) strongly disagree that Christianity is extremist; 41 percent disagree somewhat. You might say disagreeing somewhat or disagreeing strongly is the difference between "I guess not" and "Of course not!" So even among non-Christians who reject the idea that Christianity is extremist, there is a lot of ambivalence.

What happened? And what is behind the growing perception that public expression of religious conviction is extreme?

Putting "Extremism" in Context

North America is becoming more religiously plural. There are more faith groups represented among the population than there were fifty years ago, and more faith "tribes" have a significant voice in our cultural dialogue. Example: the 2012 presidential campaign of Mitt Romney would have been unthinkable five decades ago, but Mormons are no longer considered a fringe group as they once were. Muslims now comprise a significant proportion of the population of several US cities and are an even larger proportion of Europe's population. And don't forget the recent advance of atheists and their philosophical cousins, the religiously unaffiliated.

Meanwhile, the Christian share of the population has shrunk. The voice of evangelicals, for many years among the most politically and culturally resonant, sounds less persuasive to an increasing number of ears—especially to those who think religion should be always private, never public. Evangelicals' fundamental belief in the importance of sharing the gospel (a public act, if ever there was one) is seen as extreme by a majority of adults in a society trying to come to grips with religious diversity.

But it's not *only* evangelicals. We asked US adults about several minority groups, religious and otherwise. How difficult would it be for them to have a natural and normal conversation with a person from that group? As shown in the following table, a majority of Americans would struggle to have a conversation with a Muslim (73 percent), a Mormon (60 percent), an atheist (56 percent), an evangelical (55 percent), or someone from the LGBT community (52 percent).

It's interesting how often certain segments feel the difficulty of natural conversations with those on the opposite end of the faith spectrum. For example, the no-faith segment is most likely to perceive difficulty in talking with evangelicals.

Practicing Christians and evangelicals are also likely to perceive major conversational barriers. Think about it: Christians are commanded by Jesus to go and make disciples—and doing so requires conversations. It demands partnering with the Holy Spirit to have "conversations that are gracious and effective" (see Colossians 4:5–6). But for some reason, Christians are among the *most* likely to feel tension that could prevent a conversation with people who are different from them.

If Christians are to be agents of good faith, we've got to overcome the real or perceived barriers to talking with people who don't already agree with us. We need to become experts at engaging in difficult conversations.

People with Whom It's Difficult to Have a Conversation

Which groups do you think it would be difficult for you to have a natural and normal conversation with? Mark all that apply.

% "very" + "somewhat" difficult

	% US Adults	% Evan-gelicals	% Prac-ticing Christians	% Other Faiths	% Atheists, Agnostics, Unaffiliated (No Faith)	% LGBT
Muslims	73	87	81	73	63	57
Mormons	60	67	65	66	61	63
Atheists	56	85	75	38	29	39
Evangelicals	55	28*	44	69	66	58
LGBT community	52	87	74	47	39	39

Source: Barna OmniPoll, August 2015, N = 1,000

* Barna's definition of "evangelical" is based on agreement with a series of belief statements, not on self-identification. (See the Glossary for the complete definition.) Thus, not all those who qualify under Barna's definition identify themselves as "evangelical."

In broad strokes, many people think it would be difficult to have a conversation with anyone who's not a part of *their* group. Many of us, in other words, find it challenging to connect and have meaningful conversations with others.

The state of our union is one of dis-union.

The conversational health of our society is in bad shape.

As a culture, we are trying to figure out how to make sense of the widening religious and ideological differences we experience every day. Sometimes it feels like we're all in an epic tug-of-war to decide who gets to narrate reality and determine what is true and good. And, by default, the mushy middle seems to be winning. Many people are gravitating to a contrived centrist position that says everything will be okay if none of us holds too tightly to any particular belief. Ironically, this contrived center is itself becoming an ideology, as people grip it more and more tightly and call the people tugging on the ends extremists.

Given this backdrop, we can see how Christians who *do* talk about their faith threaten a fragile cultural consensus. And, make no mistake, that faith *is* a threat. Christians believe God reveals what is true and good—and are willing to keep on tugging even if everyone else disagrees.

Extremism and Difficult Conversations

An ever-increasing number of people *do* disagree, as we will see. And based on extensive research and our own experiences, we believe perceptions of extremism (and irrelevance) are creating tremendous tension in four areas. By tension we mean that good faith Christians feel pulled between their religious convictions and a desire to live at peace with others. Later chapters of this book explore these four areas, with the hope that you'll come away from *Good Faith* feeling less negative tension when it's time to engage in those difficult conversations that are a part of living in our diverse world.

By book's end we hope you'll feel more confident about what to believe, how to live in agreement with those beliefs, and how to love others whose beliefs are different.

The four areas we explore are:

1. *Neighborliness and intolerance in public life.* Christians are feeling tension as they try to engage with neighborhoods, communities, and governments. How can Christians be good neighbors? More collectively, how can their good faith efforts help to build a good society? Should they just keep their mouths shut when their views conflict with those of their friends? Many Christians, like other people of faith, are wrestling with how to live well and do good in a pluralistic culture.

2. *Relationships.* How do we live a faith that is good for human relationships? Can the church lead our communities toward sexual wholeness and racial reconciliation? Do all lives matter? We contend that deep, Spirit-filled Christian community is the only true cure for the profound relational ills that plague our culture.

3. *Sexual ethics.* Perhaps the most front-and-center perception of extremism relates to traditional Christian sexual ethics. Are Christians who are committed to an orthodox understanding of sex simply on the wrong side of history? How can single believers realistically remain chaste? How can Christians speak and act in love for LGBT people? We believe Christians can be *for* an orthodox understanding of sexuality without being *against* LGBT people, who are loved by God and created in his image.

4. *Church and religion.* What role can faith play in modern life? What role *should* it play? Is a religious community good for everyone or only those who are a part of it? We'll look at upsides and downsides of the church's past and present relationship with society and explore ideas about the future of that dynamic.

Christians have been wrestling with big concepts and real challenges like these since the time of Jesus. We don't have a secret solution that has somehow eluded thinkers and practitioners of the past. But we do hope that reliable data, careful analysis, and a commitment to understanding our times will help you know what to do today and in the years to come.

First, we need to talk candidly about what, exactly, has happened within the broader dominant culture to bring us to this moment.

4

THE TENSION WE
FEEL AND WHY

Sensationalists are easily dismissed, and for good reason: there is a lot of unwarranted fear-mongering among Christians.

Yet, in the midst of the hype, we think a very real story is not being told. Just in our two decades of work within the Christian community, things have happened that should cause concern—even if you're skeptical (like us) about the-sky-is-falling narratives.

The believers we know and work with are feeling significant pressure. This is not just a set of woe-is-me, victim-mentality perceptions that Christians have cooked up for no good reason. The society we live in has not only moved away from a Christian worldview, it has become actively antagonistic toward those who seek to advance faith. The effects are starting to be felt in tangible ways.

Every year, Barna and Q interact with tens of thousands of Christian leaders from all walks of life and from various nonprofit, business, academic, and church sectors. We speak to and consult with leaders from an ecumenical range of groups—mostly evangelical but also mainline and Catholic organizations. With our own eyes, we are seeing the facts on the ground.

We work with business leaders who report experiencing disapproval within their industry about the Christian way of life.

We know educational leaders who have heard from accrediting organizations to tread carefully in the days to come.

We are friends with pastors who are dealing with significant opposition from city and state governments; one was at the center of a case where pastors' sermons were subpoenaed by a mayor looking for ammunition to advance her agenda.

We have had long conversations with college professors and public officials who constantly have to guard what they say and how they say it, for fear of professional repercussions.

We have listened in on the pain of ministry leaders whose ministries are no longer welcome on college campuses.

We hear from Christian researchers (not us) who are black-listed if they report findings that don't align with culturally approved norms.

We know business owners who have made agonizing decisions about how to (or how not to) apply their deeply held principles in order to comply with legislation or public opinion.

We have friends who did not get jobs because of their convictions.

We regularly hear from Christian leaders who are wary of negative news coverage about their work. Even if we

acknowledge that good journalism *ought* to dig into religion's sins (clergy abuse scandals come to mind), the leaders
we serve are telling us that something is different in recent
years. Some journalists are like faith-seeking missiles, out
to find, report, and destroy.

And of course there is the ever-present threat of a social
media or PR disaster. It's a hyper-transparent world. But it's
also a world that is hypercritical of Christian leaders and
organizations.

These are just a few of the slings and arrows directed toward
Christians and Christian institutions. This is the tension so
many of us are feeling.

Having wielded considerable social power in the past by
virtue of our numbers and heritage, many Christians feel tense.
When we look at the broadest segment of practicing Christians, a group that includes Catholics, evangelicals, and mainline churchgoers, a majority says they feel "misunderstood"
(54 percent) and "persecuted" (52 percent), while millions of
others use terms like "marginalized" (44 percent), "sidelined"
(40 percent), "silenced" (38 percent), "afraid to speak up" (31
percent), and "afraid to look stupid" (23 percent) to describe
living their faith in society today. Evangelicals are even more
likely to perceive their experience of faith in culture in these
negative terms.

Although we both work with a broad base of Christian traditions, the data and our up-close work within the evangelical
community indicate these worries are intensifying. In our lines
of work—convening and educating Christian leaders (Gabe)
and conducting and analyzing research about faith and culture
(David)—we have seen concerns about these matters increase
over the last five years.

The Tension of Being a Person of Faith

Thinking about your faith, how do you feel, personally, in society today?

% "very" + "somewhat" accurate

	% US Adults	% Evangelicals	% Practicing Christians	% Practicing Christian Millennials	% Other Faiths
Misunderstood	41	65	54	65	57
Persecuted	33	60	52	60	45
Marginalized	31	53	44	48	33
Sidelined	29	48	40	59	36
Silenced	28	50	38	46	34
Afraid to speak up	23	32	31	47	22
Afraid to look stupid	19	21	23	38	19

Source: Barna OmniPoll, August 2015, *N* = 1,000
base: people who consider themselves a "person of faith"

Millennial practicing Christians, in particular, are getting hit from all sides. They are more likely than other practicing Christians to feel the negative repercussions of their faith in today's society. Most feel "persecuted" and "misunderstood," and many say they feel "afraid to speak up."

Part of the reason is the negative perceptions of their non-Christian peers, a trend we documented in *unChristian*. Another pressure point is growing skepticism about the Bible. According to research for American Bible Society, there is an increasing percentage of younger adults who are skeptical about the Bible, compared to older adults—that is, they believe the Bible is just like any other book written by men. One-quarter of non-Christian Millennials believe the Bible is a "dangerous book of religious dogma that has been used for centuries to oppress people." Thirty-eight percent believe the Bible is "mythology" and 30 percent say it is just a book of "fairy tales." When young non-Christians see someone reading the Bible, the most common perceptions are that the person is a political conservative, that he or she is old-fashioned, and that they have nothing in common with the reader.

Irrelevant and extreme.

Boomers and Elders, adults who are a little further along life's journey, are wondering if their children and grandchildren are being "lost" when it comes to faith. They feel the tension of trying to express their faith in a meaningful way when it seems to fall on deaf ears. It almost seems like the whole language has changed.

Pastors are feeling the tension too. They want to help people follow Jesus, but it is hard to disciple with lasting effect when many churchgoers show up only once or twice a month. Furthermore, churchgoers are immersed in a entertainment- and media-saturated culture that shapes their lives and lifestyles in deep, irresistible ways. Pastors tell us they worry about the commitment level of their people and their willingness to be disciples. And they confess they feel inadequate to untangle the complexities of teaching people to follow Christ in today's culture.

There is also the tension felt by various Christian traditions and institutions. For example, many denominational and parachurch organizations are being pulled apart by questions about how to respond to LGBT issues. Christian schools, colleges, universities, and seminaries are experiencing dramatic demographic, financial, and social changes, which are calling into question the sustainable future of these institutions.

The Catholic community has experienced tension for many years on issues of healthcare (such as birth control and contraception), right to life, adoption, and marriage and family, among others. Our friend Bill, a prominent Catholic leader in

Los Angeles, says, "We Catholics have long understood what it means to live as a minority in the country, and how to keep pursuing our convictions in spite of that. It hasn't been easy. And it's only getting harder!"

And then there's the tension that threatens the unity of the church. Sometimes it feels like Christianity is fragmenting into a million little pieces, whether because of outside forces—say, a journalist who describes evangelicals like they are from a distant planet—or from Christians attacking Christians. We know firsthand the pain of someone misperceiving and mischaracterizing our work and motives.

We are all feeling the tension.

But where is it from? What is causing it?

We believe the problem is our culture's lack of a shared center. The bottom has dropped out. There is no center any longer. There is a giant vacuum in the middle of our moral and spiritual lives.

We do not believe there is a massive anti-Christian conspiracy, but we do recognize a coherent and principled set of secular convictions that runs deeply counter to Christian belief. It may not be a coordinated effort, but let's not be naïve: those with a different worldview would love to fill the cultural vacuum with their notions of what is true.

This is one reason some Christians are so quick to react to Hollywood, to academia, to media elites, and so on. They have this innate sense, corroborated by what they hear from their leaders and see in the public square, that the Christian community's voice is being intentionally silenced.[1]

As Christianity has been ushered out of our social structures and off the cultural main stage, it has left a vacuum in its place. And the broader culture is trying to fill the void.

A Shared Center

If you're not sure we ever had a shared center, join us on a brief tour of history.

On March 4, 1865—about eight generations ago—newly reelected president Abraham Lincoln delivered his Second Inaugural Address. References to both the Old and the New Testament peppered the speech. Lincoln alluded to Genesis 3 in his criticism that slave owners would "ask a just God's assistance in wringing their bread from the sweat of other men's faces." He repeated Jesus's warning in Matthew 18: "Woe to that man by whom the offense cometh!" And he affirmed God's sovereignty over the nationally devastating, not-quite-over Civil War by quoting Psalm 19: "The judgments of the Lord are true and righteous altogether."[2]

The majority of President Lincoln's listeners, and of the millions across the country who read his address in newspapers, would have instantly recognized these references. There was only one English translation of the Bible at the time—the King James Version—and it was the only book some people had ever read. Its impact and influence on American culture are hard to overestimate; a century and a half ago, the KJV was "a conceptual canopy for the entire English-speaking world."[3]

But if Lincoln were to give his iconic speech today, many people would not get it—and not just because there are so many more Bible translations today than in 1865. If Lincoln delivered the Second Inaugural Address today, at least a few people would object to his use of the Bible to make his points. The fact that the entire speech is a meditation on God's will would raise some eyebrows too.

But not so long ago, using this kind of language in public life was not exceptional. Do a Google search: in just the last few decades, our nation's leaders frequently acknowledged Christianity as the "shared center." Even President Eisenhower, who may not have been a committed born-again Christian, spoke about Christianity and referred to Christian symbols with the assumption that most Americans knew what he was talking about.

Recent presidents—and not just George W. Bush, who is famously vocal about his faith—referred to Jesus as "our Savior." President Bill Clinton affirmed his belief in Jesus's miracles and resurrection, which he described as "the central event" in the history of salvation. Easter, he said, demonstrates that "good conquered evil, hope overcame despair, and life triumphed over death." He also declared, "God's only Son brought the assurance of God's love and presence in our lives and the promise of salvation." Jesus is "the true Light that illumines all humankind."[4]

Can you imagine a president making these claims today? Religious pluralism makes it difficult to have a shared basis for morality. And thanks in part to values based on the Hebrew and Christian Scriptures, the United States may be the most religiously diverse nation on the planet.[5] Ironically, that diversity makes public use of those Scriptures problematic.

If we are losing our shared center, what is filling that hole?

The New Code

For a couple centuries of American public life, a soft reliance on the state to endorse Christian values seemed to work just fine. Since most people assumed America was a "Christian nation," it made sense that federal and state laws tacitly affirmed a biblical worldview and actively promoted Christian morals. From gambling and alcohol prohibition to tax exemptions and modesty laws, nominal Christianity benevolently reigned over the public square. Everyone stayed buttoned up, and, for the most part, we appeared to be a virtuous people, a moral people.

But in the twentieth century, more and more people began to see Christian morality as standing in the way of a new moral code: the morality of self-fulfillment. Throwing off burdensome traditional mores, people began to imagine life without a bothersome God standing watch. John Lennon captured the zeitgeist in his perennial hit: "Imagine there's no heaven, it's easy if you try . . ."

New research, as shown in the next table, highlights the extent to which Americans pledge allegiance to the new moral code, summed up in six guiding principles.

1. To find yourself, look within yourself.
2. People should not criticize someone else's life choices.[6]
3. To be fulfilled in life, pursue the things you desire most.
4. Enjoying yourself is the highest goal of life.
5. People can believe whatever they want as long as those beliefs don't affect society.
6. Any kind of sexual expression between two consenting adults is fine.

The morality of self-fulfillment is everywhere, like the air we breathe. Much of the time we don't even notice we're constantly bombarded with messages that reinforce self-fulfillment—in music, movies, video games, apps, commercials, TV shows, and every other kind of media.

Web ads are a perfect (and somewhat creepy) example. You may have noticed ads on Facebook or YouTube for items you recently browsed online. When you visit a retail website, a small

The New Moral Code

Please indicate whether you agree or disagree with each of the following statements.

% "completely" + "somewhat" agree

	% US Adults	% Practicing Christians
The best way to find yourself is by looking within yourself	91	76
People should not criticize someone else's life choices	89	76
To be fulfilled in life, you should pursue the things you desire most	86	72
The highest goal of life is to enjoy it as much as possible	84	66
People can believe whatever they want, as long as those beliefs don't affect society	79	61
Any kind of sexual expression between two consenting adults is acceptable	69	40

Source: Barna OmniPoll, August 2015, *N* = 1,000

piece of data called a cookie stores itself in your browser and sends messages to other sites you visit about what you looked at and clicked on. Based on your browsing history, those sites then show you ads for things you want but haven't bought yet. And all the time, seeing those tailor-made ads out of the corner of your eye, you get the message "to be fulfilled in life, pursue the things you desire most" and "enjoying yourself is the highest goal of life."

Me-focused morality is all the rage. To see this, one only has to look at two relationships that, according to traditional Christianity, require epic levels of self-sacrifice and others-focus to do them right: marriage and parenting. Personal fulfillment has taken center stage. Culturally, marriage has become about little more than how I feel when I'm with my spouse, how he or she "completes me." And parenting is similarly me-oriented, as marketing copy from a life coaching website shows: "Parenting struggles are a perfect opportunity for personal growth. Use parenting as your path towards personal fulfillment and creating your best life!"[7] Wouldn't you love to be their kids?

As you can see in the table, the morality of self-fulfillment has even crept into American Christianity. Large percentages of practicing Christians embrace the principles of the new moral code.

Dallas Willard diagnosed this spiritual sickness in his 2009 book *Knowing Christ Today*, where he writes:

> The worldview answers people now live by are provided by feelings. Desire, not reality and not what is good, rules our world. That is even true for the most part within religion. Most of what Americans do in their religion now is done at the behest of feelings. . . . The quest for pleasure takes over the house of God. What is good or what is true is no longer the guide.[8]

Too many Christians have substituted comfortable living for a life changed by the gospel. The government's tacit endorsement of vaguely Christian morals has made it difficult, in many ways, to discern what it means to be faithful, beyond showing up.

In recent years, the morality of self-fulfillment has begun to bear its inevitable fruit: people want to fulfill themselves by doing things outside the bounds of cultural Christianity. And they don't want the law telling them they can't.

As a result of this shift, we are seeing laws that endorse the broader culture's replacement of Christian morality with the moral code of self-fulfillment. And according to that moral code, any competing morality—say, a religion—that seeks to constrain someone's pursuit of personal fulfillment must itself be constrained.

If something or someone stands in the way of my fulfillment, that obstacle must be removed. That person represents the enemy, the embodiment of evil. So keep your beliefs to yourself.

God's Moral Order

In contrast to the dominant culture's embrace of self-fulfillment as the highest good, good faith Christians believe living under God's moral order leads to human and societal flourishing. As Scripture says, physical training is of some benefit, but "training for godliness is much better, promising benefits in this life and in the life to come" (1 Tim. 4:8).

Yet the extent to which the morality of self-fulfillment has taken hold of the hearts and minds of practicing Christians exposes an area of dangerous weakness in today's church. This grafting of cultural dogma onto Christian theology must stop. In order for us to flourish as God's people, his moral order must be allowed to rule our lives.

What are the principles of God's moral order? Contrasting the new moral code are six statements about the way life ought to be, with Jesus at the center.

1. To find yourself, discover the truth *outside* yourself, in Jesus.
2. Loving others does not always mean staying silent.
3. Joy is found not in pursuing our own desires but in giving of ourselves to bless others.
4. The highest goal of life is giving glory to God.
5. God gives people the freedom to believe whatever they want, but those beliefs always affect society.
6. God designed boundaries for sex and sexuality in order for humans to flourish.

We've purposely expressed these six principles as a response to the six principles of the new moral code. Christians express something truly *counter*cultural when we insist that real morality is rooted in something outside ourselves. Even if it feels uncomfortable at first, we have an obligation, in good faith, to speak as a counterculture to the spirit of the age. Beyond using our voices, we need to do the hard work of being countercultural in our own lives and churches. Only when we are consistent will our lives stir outsiders to rethink their own moral compass.

Living counter to the new morality is an uphill battle. Some days it feels like keeping the wind from blowing. Nearly everything about the broader culture is expertly marketed to appeal to our comfort, well-being, safety, and satisfaction. A delicious meal. Your dream holiday. The perfect house. Great sex. What will fulfill you? For ages, humans have bent toward self-indulgence. In our advertising age, there are countless ways of making people crave.

But then there is the way of Jesus. The Westminster Catechism's first question asks, "What is the chief end of man?" The answer, as generations of Protestant confirmands could tell you, is "to glorify God and enjoy him forever." There are profound moral implications here. If the highest goal of life is God's glory rather than our own enjoyment, then our outward behaviors and inward character will have a drastically different shape.

Conversations about Morality

Regardless of whether it's popular, and perhaps especially when it is not, we advocate for the biblical and historical Christian view of morality. We believe God's moral order leads to human flourishing.

Because the new morality is not a better way to live, it inevitably leads to dead ends. When this happens, where will people turn? If we are burning the flame of God's moral order bright, they will have a beacon to follow out of the darkness. If we aren't, and we are only trying to keep up with culture's latest trends, we will have nothing to offer.

You may be thinking, *What if the historic Christian faith is on the wrong side of history? What if, by following the trail blazed by earlier generations of believers, we are getting some things wrong?*

These are reasonable questions, and we will take a closer look at some answers in chapters ahead. Still, we believe history is a great guide. History helps us gain perspective, especially on the biggest competing ideas of our time. Understanding history helps us set this moment in context, to see that this current competition of ideas is nothing new. It's actually quite old.

Jesus came on the scene at a time when this same old idea we contend with today was gaining traction.

Roughly one hundred years before Christ's birth, a Roman philosopher named Lucretius wrote an epic poem called "On the Nature of Things." Through this stunning work of art, Lucretius made an argument for *pleasure* as the ultimate purpose of human life. We exist to enjoy life. Nothing more, nothing less. Good living all the time. Avoid pain at all costs and pursue pleasure in any way you can.[9]

Sound familiar? (See principles 2, 3, and 4 of the new moral code.)

Lucretius is the father of YOLO, "you only live once." And the last fifty years have made the dominant culture ripe for a revival of his pleasure-centered philosophy.

Now, don't hear us wrong. Nothing is bad about enjoying God's good world, but when it becomes the ultimate focus, we've become our own god. Ancient as it is, this is the crux of the new morality. This is the reason Christians are on the outs with the dominant culture. To an increasing number of people, our insistence that pleasure and self-fulfillment are destructive isn't just irrelevant or extreme.

It is evil.

If your friends have bought into the idea that self-fulfillment is the ultimate purpose of life, then you or anyone else who stands in their way is evil. So sit down, shut up, and keep your faith to yourself.

But this isn't the way of Jesus.

Several decades later, in a glaring yet gentle contrast to Lucretius's philosophy, came Jesus, who taught that *renewal*—redemption, restoration, re-creation—is God's purpose for every human life. Pain, brokenness, and suffering are not to be avoided; they are to be endured because God redeems those experiences in order to renew us and bless others.

We contend that these two vastly different narratives are at war today. Instead of a culture war, we are engaged in a struggle over the human imagination. Two visions of life are playing out before our eyes.

One is a good belief and leads to life.

The other is a bad idea and leads to death.

When we feel the cultural winds blowing against us, let's be reminded how long the moral ideas of the Christian faith have rolled on—no matter their competition in each successive age. Rest assured, good faith is on the right side of history.

Through the power of the Holy Spirit at work in us, Christians can confront the culture with a better way to live—the way of renewal, not of self-fulfillment. By grace we have been given the center our culture is missing. But good faith Christians must become communicators—translators really—who can effectively challenge the self-fulfillment and pleasure-seeking spirit of the age in written, spoken, artistic, and other forms.

Of course, first we have to *love* our neighbors enough to offer this better way and *believe* that Jesus's narrative truly is the best way to live the human story. And then, in spite of the tension we feel, we must *live* the way of renewal when we rub shoulders with some of the most urgent moral questions of our day.

Let's start with a simple (but not easy) formula for good faith: love, believe, live.

PART II

LIVING GOOD FAITH

5

LOVE, BELIEVE, LIVE

Good faith Christians are a
counterculture for the common good.

Given the challenges Christians face, from both outside and inside the church, living with good faith is our way forward into an uncertain future. We must be the people of God who, rather than being defined only by what we are *against*, are also defined by what we are *for*.

There are so many good faith Christians who often go unheralded. Consider how these Christians and organizations are living out good faith in their communities.

Lisa Jo encourages moms through her blogging and writing in Virginia.

Jim talks about Jesus in natural, unforced ways with his house-painting customers in Seattle.

Mission Year provides students with an opportunity to serve together for one year for the benefit of a city neighborhood and then to incorporate what they learn into their future lives.

Jeff teaches high school students in Denver to love C. S. Lewis.

Ruth brings her faith to work styling clients' hair in Edinburgh, Scotland.

Simon and Marianne adopted two kids with learning and behavioral difficulties near London, England.

Southlake Church in Portland, Oregon, began a national Churches Adopting Schools program that is reshaping how Christians invest in local education.

Tarien helps teenagers create art and learn to design in Johannesburg, South Africa.

Lori lives and works among Muslims in a place she can't divulge.

The New York communities of Trinity Grace Church support Sarah Frazier's South Bronx–based House on Beekman, which serves children living under the poverty line.

Ben leads a team that rescues modern-day slaves, victims of human trafficking, in Manchester, England.

Josh has developed a reputation in Phoenix for encouraging his fellow college students to pray and study the Scriptures.

Jessica helps young families reimagine their quality time together in Boston.

In Sydney, Australia, Mike supports Christians enduring persecution in places where being a Christian isn't just extreme or irrelevant but illegal.

Jill is the school sports photographer and prayer supporter and is raising three Jesus-loving kids in Ventura, California.

Rebekah is shaping three young souls too and writes books in Nashville, Tennessee.

(Disclosure: Jill and Rebekah are the best moms, and wives, on the planet.)

All of these people and millions more are faithfully doing the thing the Lord has put in front of them—whether big, small, or in between—regardless of whether they get credit or kudos. This is living in good faith.

We have covered much about our cultural context, problems, and areas of confusion in the previous chapters. Now we want to lay out a few big ideas to help Christians stake all of this conceptual stuff to the ground.

Talking about good faith is nice, but how do we know if we're getting it right?

The Bible and Good Faith

Nobody debates whether "good" means something beneficial or whether "doing good" is a worthy aim. Everyone wants "good" in the world. But our individual definitions of good, and means of achieving it, differ by a wide mile.

To arrive at a *Christian* understanding of good, we start with the Bible. We want God to be the source of our notions about good, so we need a biblically grounded picture of what we're shooting for when we say we want to be people of good faith.

You might be surprised to find that good is a common theme in the Bible. One of our favorite verses, and one that effectively captures the theme of this book, is from Hebrews:

"Let us think of ways to motivate one another to acts of love and good works" (10:24).

But good goes back much, much further in God's story. In fact, we find good at the very beginning—when the Creator surveys his handiwork and sees that it is good (see Gen. 1). We see in the biblical account of God's earliest work in the world a picture of what he means by good: his creation is orderly and right, abundant and generous, beautiful and flourishing with life and relationships.

The New Testament echoes the theme that the people of God are to be agents of good. For example:

- In the Sermon on the Mount, Jesus tells his listeners, "Let your good deeds shine out for all to see, so that everyone will praise your heavenly Father" (Matt. 5:16).
- Paul returns to the words *good* and *goodness* many times in his letters to the early churches. "Let God transform you into a new person . . . then you will learn to know God's will for you, which is good and pleasing and perfect" (Rom. 12:2); "God causes everything to work together for the good" (8:28); "the Kingdom of God is not a matter of what we eat or drink, but of living a life of goodness and peace and joy in the Holy Spirit" (14:17); "the Holy Spirit produces this kind of fruit in our lives: love, joy, peace, patience, kindness, goodness, faithfulness, gentleness, and self-control" (Gal. 5:22–23); "let's not get tired of doing what is good" (6:9); "we are God's masterpiece. He has created us anew in Christ Jesus, so we can do the good things he planned for us long ago" (Eph. 2:10). There are so many more.
- Peter tells persecuted Christians in the early days of the church, "You can show others the goodness of God, for

he called you out of the darkness into his wonderful light" (1 Pet. 2:9).

- And the apostle James, of course, could not be more blunt when he writes, "Faith is dead without good works" (2:26) and "If you are wise and understand God's ways, prove it by living an honorable life, doing good works with the humility that comes from wisdom" (3:13).

What does this brief overview show us? It ought to hit us between the eyes that good *is for the benefit of others*. Although these verses are from the New Testament, good is a theme as old as the covenant God made with Abraham: blessed to be a blessing (see Gen. 12). Gabe's work in the last few years has focused a great deal on helping Christians understand our calling and responsibility to be restorers. In and through Christ, we are to be agents of restoration, putting right the effects of a broken, bent, and disordered world.

Living in good faith means helping the world and the people in it to be orderly and right, abundant and generous, beautiful and flourishing with life and relationships—just as God created them to be.

Good.

But this brings us to a second point about good according to Scripture: we have no real ability to be or to generate good on our own. "Whatever is good . . . is a gift coming down to us from God our Father" (James 1:17). This means that good works done with wrong motives can still have a positive impact. The effect of hot food on a hungry person doesn't depend on our motivation. The road to irrelevance is paved with overthinking.

At the same time, when it comes to maturing in good faith, motivation matters a great deal. If we are trying to "motivate one another to acts of love and good works" for the sake of our own reputation, to make ourselves look good, to generate positive publicity, or to make people like us more, we are getting good wrong. Our good works should cause others to praise the Father, not us. If we are trying to do good works to make ourselves worthy of God's love, we are getting good wrong. Our good works should be a response of selfless love toward others in thanks for Jesus's unconditional love for us.

With these biblical perspectives on good in mind, let's turn to how we can make good our faith in Jesus.

Love, Believe, Live

If you are a chef, you know that to make a great dish you need the right ingredients. Ever tasted a cake missing a key ingredient? Ugh! It just plain tastes bad.

Good faith relies on three essential ingredients. Skip any of them and it goes sour. Unfortunately, a lot of faith walking around these days just plain tastes bad.

The secret recipe for good faith boils down to this: how well you *love*, what you *believe*, and how you *live*. If you don't have all three, your faith isn't good—it's half-baked. This may sound judgmental or harsh to otherwise well-meaning believers, but we mean these words in the most caring way possible. We care about the Christian community and sincerely believe good faith in today's cultural climate requires all three ingredients.

Love

Good faith starts with loving God and loving others—the great commandment. Jesus summarizes God's law like this: love God with all your heart, all your soul, and all your mind, and love other people as yourself (see Matt. 22:37–40). Our friend Steve Garber says Christians' biggest challenge today is that we've learned to love the wrong things. So true! We need rightly ordered love to be people of good faith.

When we are missing the ingredient of love, we lack humility. We all know Christians who believe the right things and appear to live faithfully, but their arrogance is abrasive and off-putting. "I'm just telling the straight truth," they say, as though truth needs an adjective. If we're honest with ourselves, each of us who holds orthodox belief in high regard struggles with this from time to time. We must be wary of becoming like the self-righteous religious leaders of Jesus's day who hijacked God's revelation to suit their own purposes.

Thinking about our earlier definition of good, we might say that one indicator of a lack of love is a laser-like focus on good as orderly and right to the exclusion of the other equally important facets of biblical goodness. We may be orderly and right, but, as Paul says, without love we're a noisy gong or a clanging cymbal (see 1 Cor. 13:1).

Believe

The next ingredient of good faith is biblical orthodoxy. What we believe matters. The two of us are committed Jesus-followers, so it should come as no surprise that we believe the Christian take on reality represents "the most comprehensive life system that answers all of humanity's age-old questions."[1] We believe Christianity makes the most sense of the beauty (God's design) and the horror (the fall) of human experience. Understanding and believing the creation-fall-redemption-restoration story at the heart of Christian orthodoxy help us make sense of where we come from, what's wrong, how we can fix it, and what our purpose is in this world. To people of good faith, theology matters. It allows us to identify and correct distortions in the world, in the church, and in our own thinking. (We are committed evangelicals and claim a particular theological tradition,[2] but in this book, we aim to be as broadly orthodox as possible so that mainline, Orthodox, and Catholic believers can adapt and apply these ideas to their traditions as well.)

When we don't believe rightly, we are confused or outright mistaken about God's intent for human flourishing. We embrace distortions about God, humanity, or the world. To give an extreme example, many people sincerely believe that pornography is simply a normal expression of human sexuality. This belief is either true or it's not. (It's not.) Many people, even many Christians, honestly believe that sex before marriage is a healthy sexual choice. This belief is either true or it's not. (It's not.)

There is a difference between good beliefs (orderly, right, flourishing with life and relationships) and bad ideas.

Discerning the difference has nothing to do with loving people, and we must avoid the temptation to base our beliefs on how we think they might sound to others. Younger Christians, in particular, seem to be tempted in this way, to embrace a distorted truth in order to maintain a friendship. But good love and good belief can and do coexist. (This is where the third ingredient comes in.) In fact, without good belief, we can't know for certain how to love people well.

Live

Finally, how we live our love and belief is the third ingredient of good faith. How do we translate our love and our beliefs into everyday living? Are our interactions with people a clear reflection of our love for God and others? Do we understand the implications of orthodoxy for how we live, work, and relate?

This ingredient is crucial, the one that ties the whole recipe together.

When we don't have a coherent pattern of living, one that expresses both good love and good belief, we lack confidence that faith matters in the world and feel incapable of bringing love and orthodoxy to bear on everyday life. You probably know Christians who seem to lack the language or the tools they need to engage the world around them. They genuinely love others. They believe the right things. But they don't know how to channel their love and belief from heart and head into their daily lives.

No one can have good faith without this recipe.

How well we love + What we believe + How we live = Good Faith

When we combine the perfect mix of all three, our faith is good.

Good Faith Is Countercultural

When communities of Jesus-followers commit to living good faith, the results can be summed up like this: Christians are a counterculture for the common good. Being countercultural, in this definition, is not only about addressing age-old issues from a gospel-centered perspective. It's not about raising our voices to drown out dissenters or making laws to make everyone behave nicely. It's not about plastering Jesus's name across billboards and T-shirts or creating a "Christian" alternative to every secular product or service. While some well-intentioned believers take these approaches, by "countercultural" we mean something different.

Being countercultural means bringing good faith—a vision for what is orderly and right, abundant and generous, beautiful and flourishing with life and relationships—to the broader culture. This vision is not just an individual pursuit; it is best expressed in communities of faith where believers love and care for one another well and then invite others in to experience the same grace.

Christians and churches that live this way find not only that their faith becomes more alive but also that their collective impact on their communities is deeper. In our research, the results of which are shown in the table, large majorities of practicing Christians, especially Millennials and evangelicals, report two confident attitudes. They feel they are "a force for good," and they feel they are "essential." In other words, if they were to go away, their communities would notice.

This is the fruit of living good faith.

Good Faith in Society

Thinking about your faith, how do you feel, personally, in society today?

% "very" + "somewhat" accurate

	% US Adults	% Evangelicals	% Practicing Christians	% Practicing Christian Millennials	% Other Faiths
A force for good	88	98	93	91	88
Accepted	81	57	78	74	61
Essential	75	93	86	77	76
Empowered	69	71	78	81	76
Distinctive	60	86	76	73	72
Countercultural	31	42	40	62	31

Source: Barna OmniPoll, August 2015, N = 1,000
base: people who consider themselves a "person of faith"

Interestingly, *countercultural* is the word Christians identify with least among the options—yet even still, 42 percent
of evangelicals, 40 percent of practicing Christians, and a
whopping 62 percent of practicing Christian Millennials
say this is a "very" or "somewhat" accurate description of
their feelings related to their faith in society. We fervently
pray that these numbers will grow during the next decade as
more Jesus-followers understand that being countercultural
doesn't mean condemning but offering a better way, as we
described above.

Jesus offers us a vivid picture of being countercultural in his
parable of the good Samaritan recorded in Luke 10:30–37. (He
didn't give the story its title, by the way.) After two thousand
years of Christians reading, preaching, and telling this story to
children, it has morphed from a countercultural shock wave
into a nice morality tale about being kind to others. But the day
he told it, in response to the question "Who is my neighbor?"
it was nothing less than a category-redefining mind shift for
his listeners.

Minds were blown.

Jesus's response to the question was a far-fetched tale of two
men divided by race, religion, and politics brought together
when one of them came with the biblical idea of good to the
side of the road where the other lay dying. He got off his donkey
and started restoring the broken, bent, and disordered man in
the ditch. Which is all very wonderful and life affirming and
made-for-TV-movie . . . *except the good man is not us.*

The one who brings orderly, right, abundant, generous,
beautiful, and flourishing goodness to a broken man is the
person we would least expect. To a Christian audience of today,
Jesus might have said the good Samaritan is a bisexual, atheist,

burlesque dancer with one of those Darwin-amphibians-eating-a-Jesus-fish bumper stickers.

And the broken man is us.

It's really not a very nice story.

Before we can run around doing good, we must acknowledge our need to be healed and restored. That kind of humility is at the heart of good faith. Loving well, believing rightly, and living out our love and belief start here. If we can get that right, we're ready to tackle the tricky, treacherous issues that threaten to derail good conversations when people of faith live at the intersection of good love and right belief.

6

THE RIGHT QUESTIONS

Good faith Christians engage
culture by asking what is wrong,
what is confused, what is
right, and what is missing.

One Sunday afternoon shortly after we moved to New York, the street in front of our Manhattan apartment shut down. Instead of yellow taxis rushing by our window, I could see an inflated bounce house in the middle of the street. Free hot dogs, cookies, and a game of kiddie-pool go fish had taken over our eastside lane.

"Rebekah, did you see this? Our entire street is closed off. Let's get outside. The kids will love it!" After we made our way out, we noticed the local church was responsible for the block party. It was pretty cool and encouraging to see a church in New York serving the neighborhood. For us, it was an impromptu opportunity to meet a few neighbors—a welcoming party of sorts. (We chose to think of it that way at least.)

As the kids worked their way over to the inflatable, a fellow dad, with a British accent, walked up and said with a sarcastic laugh, "This is the *one* good thing the Christian church does every year." As if hoping to bond over the criticism, he went on, "The Christians aren't good for much else. So what brings your family to New York?"

I was about to break an unspoken rule of Manhattan life: don't discuss faith (especially the Christian faith) in public or private with a stranger. It's a major party foul, particularly at a block party and when making a first impression. But I didn't ask for it; this conversation just came begging.

Face flushing, I said, "I write books, speak, and lead an organization that helps Christians know how to advance good in their communities. We call it Q."

"Oh, okay. So . . . you are one of the Christians?"

"Yes, I am."

Recovering his confidence, he responded, "Does that Q stand for queer?"

I laughed. "No, but we are a pretty odd bunch doing our best to relate the claims of Jesus to the world we live in today. The Q stands for 'questions.' What's your name anyway?"

"Clive."

"Nice to meet you, Clive. I'm Gabe. I get why you may not like Christians. We haven't always been the best at demonstrating the ways of Jesus."

Listening More than Talking

You probably have a friend, or at least an acquaintance, like Clive. As the research shows, their perspective on the value of a church is pretty common these days. (Three out of ten Americans of no faith say a church is *not* a benefit to a community, and another three out of ten don't know if it is or isn't.) As a Christian leader, I rarely hear what people actually think. Fortunately, Clive didn't know who he was talking to when he shared his honest opinion, so I got to hear his thoughts without the varnish of good manners.

When I acknowledged the fair criticisms Christians need to own, Clive relaxed and knew I was safe—not "religious." But I was conflicted. The Christian faith has done so much good in the world, but as we described earlier, most people today have all but forgotten about it. I dislike leading off every conversation with apologies, yet it seems like the only way to an authentic conversation about faith.

That afternoon Clive and I began a friendship. We trekked through coffee shops, enjoyed impromptu stoop-side chats, and occasionally went together to social events. The more we got to know each other, the more clearly we saw all we had in common. Although Clive is a self-proclaimed agnostic, that didn't stop us from practicing true tolerance for each other. We listened to each other's thoughts even if we disagreed. We could discuss any social issue, no matter how controversial. We even worked together to serve our homeless friend Louis, who was wheelchair-bound and panhandled on our street corner. We'd make sure he was taken care of, especially when the weather turned bitterly cold.

What Clive and I have is a genuine friendship, one that sees past differences and looks for our commonalities.

To this day, he still refers to me as "you Christians." And when something is going well in his world, he exclaims, "Your God must be listening!"—acknowledging our difference with respectful, but humorous, admiration.

In order to gain trust and credibility with those who are skeptical, and to demonstrate our love for them, good faith Christians need to learn how to listen well. Good conversations don't begin with proclamations but rather by meeting people right where they are.

The Right Questions

In leading our respective organizations (Barna and Q), we have found ourselves occasionally perplexed by the way Christians—in the name of Jesus Christ—engage our culture. At times, we've been embarrassed. Of course more and more Christians feel the pressure to speak up and stand out for what we believe. But if we don't check our posture in the process, we can do more damage than good to God's mission in the world. Love is the preeminent godly virtue, and it must motivate how we live out our beliefs.

At other times, we've been delighted and deeply encouraged by how confident followers of Jesus have embraced their unique mission in our time. Theirs is a distinctive outlook, confident and clear about how to engage the mission of God in changing times. They recognize there are no words that can substitute for an encounter with the Holy Spirit. "My message and my preaching were very plain," Paul wrote in 1 Corinthians. "Rather than using clever and persuasive speeches, I relied only on the power of the Holy Spirit. I did this so you would not trust in human wisdom but in the power of God" (2:4–5).

Over the past few years, with input from friends like Pastor Jon Tyson at Trinity Grace Church and Pete Richardson of the Paterson Institute, I have tried to develop a model for how Christians can think well about and act in faithfulness when engaging our culture. As you might expect from the guy who founded Q, the theme revolves around asking the right questions. The model invites us to think long-term about our approach while being faithful to respond in the moment when something is clearly going wrong. The following four questions, and the answers, can help you challenge yourself and your community to demonstrate good faith with conviction, compassion, and creativity.

Q. What is wrong?

A. Stop and confront.

In recent history, "What is wrong?" is one question Christians have had no problem answering. Anything that offends us receives quick criticism, even condemnation. In our earlier book, *unChristian*, in fact, we unpacked the claim that many people believe Christians are the most judgmental people they've ever encountered.[1]

So what's new about this question for today? Nothing really, except *how* we respond. When Christians find something that is wrong—unjust, immoral, or outright evil—we must stop and confront it. But *how* we confront what is wrong will make all the difference.

A few years ago journalist Kirsten Powers lived this in her vocation. When the story about Dr. Kermit Gosnell of Philadelphia was developing, she was one of the first to call out the news media for not covering it. Kirsten is a self-described liberal Democrat, but she knew the evil story of a doctor killing three infants born alive during attempted abortions must be told, even if it made people uncomfortable. In a *USA Today* piece early on in the story's development, she called out the media for not giving the story the airtime it deserved. "Infant beheadings. Severed baby feet in jars. A child screaming after it was delivered alive during an abortion procedure. Haven't heard about these sickening accusations? It's not your fault. Since the murder trial of Pennsylvania abortion doctor Kermit Gosnell began March 18, there has been precious little coverage of the case that should be on every news show and front page."[2]

This was a bold move because many in her industry and political party are pro-choice abortion advocates. She risked her relationships and reputation to stop and confront their silence.

The response to her piece was moving. Over the next several days, every major news outlet began leading with the story at the top of their news broadcasts. You likely know about this horrific injustice only because of Kirsten Powers—a person who put good faith into practice.

Q. What is confused?

A. Clarify and compel.

When there is confusion about key issues in our society, Christians ought to bring *clarity* to a situation and then *compel* others to act. Most Americans would acknowledge not knowing what to do about major global crises like the Ebola epidemic or the refugee crisis in the Middle East and across Europe. Even so, as Christians, we are called to bring clarity out of the confusion. The enemy loves a confused church (and society). He likes nothing better than to keep us feeling overwhelmed by the magnitude of the problems, cowering in our corners, ineffective and despondent.

Good faith Christian Jeremy Courtney, who lives with his family in Iraq, is not confused. Having committed to serving Iraqis during the war, he moved to Baghdad and began helping children receive life-saving heart surgeries. In a place where there was no quality medical care, especially for children, he and his team have saved countless lives.

In the summer of 2014, when the ISIS threat began to arise throughout northern Iraq and Christian persecution headlined the news, Jeremy was on the ground to clearly communicate what was taking place. He was the first to help Christian leaders recognize the complexity of the situation. It wasn't only Christians being persecuted. Yezidis and Shia and Sunni Muslims were also being killed, tortured, or forced to flee from their villages. Anyone who did not pledge allegiance to the radical Islamist ISIS mandate—including Muslims—was under threat, and it was critical for Christians to know these facts. Otherwise we might play into the ISIS goal of leading a Christian-versus-Muslim holy war.

Blogger, *New York Times* bestselling author, and friend of ours, Ann Voskamp, became aware of the situation by visiting northern Iraq for herself. Jeremy hosted her with the intention of helping Ann get a better understanding of those who were fleeing the ISIS threat. They spent time in refugee camps in northern Iraq and heard the stories of young girls and families who had lost everything. Her confusion about what was happening was clarified, and Ann was compelled to act—and to invite others to do so.

When she returned, she immediately leveraged her talent (writing) to share what she had seen. Ann knew there was a lot of confusion around what the church could or should do to help. So she clarified and asked her readers to get involved and make a difference. She compelled people to act: "Defy evil with love. Defy trafficking by trafficking hope. The world needs people who defy cynical indifference by making a critical difference—and that could be us."[3]

The result was over $1.2 million raised in a matter of days. Funds were wired to Preemptive Love Coalition,[4] Jeremy Courtney's organization in Iraq, to provide much-needed medicine, food supplies, education, and investment for women to begin new businesses, even while living in transition. All of this was possible because a couple of good faith Christians decided to bring clarity to a very confused situation and to compel the faith community to act.

Q. What is right?

A. Celebrate and cultivate.

This is the fun one. You might think we Christians would be really good at celebrating good things, but it seems to be the place we need the most improvement.

We should be the very best at spotting what's good. Our taste for goodness should be so well cultivated that, whenever orderly, right, abundant, generous, and flourishing work is on display, we call it out, support it, and encourage it. Even if it doesn't come from a Christian.

Herein lies our problem. Many Christians are inclined to believe we should celebrate only good things labeled "Christian." Or we should celebrate only good work that results in conversions or personal salvation. This view reflects an underdeveloped theology of common grace.

In his classic book *How Now Shall We Live?*, the great Chuck Colson encourages Christians to have a more robust view of God's work in the world:

Evangelism and cultural renewal are *both* divinely ordained duties. God exercises his sovereignty in two ways: through *saving grace* and *common grace*. We are all familiar with saving grace; it is the means by which God's power calls people who are dead in their trespasses and sins to new life in Christ. As God's servants, we may at times be agents of his saving grace, evangelizing and bringing people to Christ. But few of us really understand common grace, which is the means by which God's power sustains creation, holding back the sin and evil that result from the Fall and that would otherwise overwhelm his creation like a great flood. As agents of God's common grace, we are called to help sustain and renew his creation, to uphold the created institutions of family and society, to pursue science and scholarship, to create works of art and beauty, and to heal and help those suffering from the results of the Fall.[5]

Celebrating and cultivating anything and everything that is good and right is part of our call as Christians, even when that goodness is springing from someone other than a Christian. Too often, when a non-Christian solves a great injustice, produces a great work of art, or helps people overcome evil, we silently think it's interesting but are careful not to celebrate it. Why? Do we fear God isn't getting the credit, so we don't want to add our voice to it?

Our friends at *Paste* magazine, led by editor Josh Jackson, are great examples of calling out goodness. They created an entire brand based on celebrating the "signs of life in music, film, and culture." Because good faith motivates their work, they've become experts at spotting and celebrating the good.

Or consider designer and fashion mogul Sid Mashburn, who created a brand that celebrates his tailors. Most design shops place these hardworking craftspeople in the back room, out of sight. But in Atlanta, Sid celebrates their hard work and their giftedness at creating beautiful suits. They do their work on the showroom floor for all to see and celebrate. As a good faith Christian, Sid values the dignity of every worker and wants those who encounter his designs to do so as well.

The film *Selma* tells the story of Martin Luther King Jr. and his leadership of the Civil Rights march from Selma to Montgomery, Alabama. Does it make a difference whether a Christian produced, directed, or acted in the film? No. This work of art is a good and true story that must be told. There is a long list of films full of truth and goodness, and Christians should be first in line to support and celebrate these works.

Think of rap artist Lecrae, who recently won a Grammy for his brilliant hip-hop music. In the often misogynistic and violent world of rap, he is a light that tells the truth about goodness in the world. Fans have responded, including many peers who have since collaborated with him on new projects. Lecrae doesn't shy away from being honest about things that are wrong, but he also knows how to celebrate goodness wherever he finds it.

Pope Francis isn't afraid to engage any person, topic, or issue, and his joyful embrace of children, disabled people, and prisoners marks him as a person who sees good wherever he goes, even where others easily overlook it. When he visited the US last year, Barna asked people their opinion of him. One out of five Americans said, "Pope Francis has caused me to make changes to my spiritual life." Among Millennials and Gen-Xers, that statistic was one out of three. It's not *only* the pope's ability to recognize and celebrate goodness that endears him to so many. But it certainly doesn't hurt.

These examples may feel out of reach, but don't let that intimidate you. Everyone who is earnestly seeking to serve Jesus can do Kingdom things. Finding goodness in the world around us opens doors and begins relationships. Consider your own neighborhood, school, or city. Who are the unsung heroes working in your community to do good? Find and celebrate them. Who is working for justice so more people can flourish? Who is caring for those with special needs or coaching the peewee baseball, hockey, or football league? Pat them on the back, send them a note of encouragement, and thank them for the good they do. In an age of selfishness and self-infatuation, their lives stand in stark contrast to the prevailing ethos and help others see a better way.

Let's learn from these examples and become known by what we are for.

Let's acknowledge the common grace and goodness happening all around us.

Let's trust God to use his image-bearers for his good purposes, even if they don't recognize him.

Q. What is missing?

A. Create and catalyze.

This question is often the hardest to answer. To point out what is missing in the world requires imagination. As poet David Rowbotham wrote, "Imagination precedes fact"—and he was right.[6] New forms of culture—not-for-profit organizations, art, business, music, film, schools, clubs, magazines, books, and on and on—cannot be created unless someone first imagines them.

This is where good faith Christians have a stunning advantage over those without faith. We've been given a glimpse into the future, which can and should shape our imaginations as we partner with God in his work to renew all things. Tim Keller says that Revelation 21 and 22 make it clear that "the ultimate purpose of redemption is not to escape the material world, but to renew it. God's purpose is not only saving individuals, but also inaugurating a new world based on justice, peace, and love, not power, strife and selfishness."[7] In the end, brokenness, injustice, violence, greed, lust, and all sin and its effects will be overcome, wiped out so the world can be re-created in harmony with God's original intent.

This vision of the future should infect how we imaginatively engage our work, relationships, and society. We can walk forward with hope and joy because we know the good ending to the story we are living in.

God has chosen to work through us despite our shortcomings. He wants us to take bold, imaginative steps of faith that offer the world a vision for how things *ought* to be.

Sarah Dubbeldam did just that. Tired of seeing the way women were portrayed and displayed across the covers and pages of magazines, she imagined the way it ought to be. She knew the value of women is so much more than perfect makeup, tiny waist size, and eye-popping cleavage. So much was wrong, but Sarah decided not to focus on condemning it. Instead, she created something. She imagined a better way and made it a reality.

Four years ago Sarah founded *Darling* magazine, a quarterly magazine that celebrates "the art of being a woman." She committed to never retouch photos (even though they conduct more than thirty photo shoots for each issue). Everything in

Darling would be 100 percent authentic. Sarah wants her magazine to offer women the opportunity to "discover beauty apart from vanity, influence apart from manipulation, style apart from materialism, sweetness apart from passivity, and womanhood without degradation."[8] She saw a distortion, imagined a better way, and then created something that was missing.

Now, in Anthropologie stores nationwide, Barnes & Noble, and several high-end designer boutiques, *Darling* is the magazine of choice on their shelves. Sarah's leadership and creativity are catalyzing a deeper conversation among women and in her industry. Women appreciate a magazine that is honest about their roles in the world, and that respects their intellect and isn't trying to profit by selling unattainable perfection but instead celebrates the beauty in women who are "not just here, but here for a purpose."[9]

Ask yourself, *What is missing?* How has God uniquely gifted or positioned you to create something or support someone who is imagining a new and better way? As Andy Crouch says, "The only way to change culture is to create culture."[10]

May we be the kind of good faith Christians who shape the future by asking the right questions and then confronting what is wrong, clarifying what is confused, celebrating what is good, and creating what the world is missing. Relying on God's guidance, you never know where these questions may lead.

Maybe right into the Oval Office.

7

WHO WILL LEAD?

Good faith Christians make space
for people who disagree.

"Can I get you coffee or tea?" our host inquired as we walked
into the room.

Already tense, I (Gabe) was taken aback at the offer and
promptly refused. "No, I'm fine, thanks."

I lowered myself onto an overstuffed caramel-colored couch
and nearly kicked myself for being an idiot. Did I really think
President Barack Obama was offering to personally make me
a cup of tea?

I forgot that presidents have butlers.

My jitters were understandable. I think I would have been
nervous even if we'd been there just to shoot hoops with the

president of the United States—but we weren't. The occasion that brought us together was a serious and, we hoped, fruitful conversation about affirming the freedom of people of faith to live out their beliefs.

The week before, President Obama had appeared on *ABC News* for a sit-down interview with Robin Roberts. On national television, he affirmed for the first time his public support for gay marriage.

Just a few years earlier, during the 2008 presidential campaign, then-candidate Obama had defended traditional marriage in an interview with Pastor Rick Warren. He said, "I believe that marriage is the union between a man and a woman. Now, for me as a Christian . . . it is also a sacred union. God's in the mix."[1] He had always been supportive of civil unions for gay couples, but he was careful to clarify the unique bond of covenant marriage between one man and one woman.

But in this month of May four years later, all that changed. The president's conversion was emblematic of a sea change sweeping the nation and foreshadowed the Supreme Court's *Obergefell* decision in 2015.

We hadn't come to talk about gay marriage. I think we recognized, even then, that the tide was turning against those of us who hoped the historic Christian vision of marriage would continue to have an honored place in the public square.

No, we had come to discuss the rights of good faith Americans to swim upstream against the cultural current. This was our one objective: to persuade the president that faithful citizens who disagree with new cultural norms must be able to exercise their beliefs in their daily lives—including in their churches, religious institutions, and engagements with the public square.

Anxiety about religious freedom is on the rise, and not just among Christians. In late summer 2015, Barna polled US adults on their perceptions of religious freedom, using a question we first asked in 2012. As the table shows, across the board, every population segment—including the "nones"—showed an upsurge in the belief that religious freedom has weakened over the past ten years.

Perceptions of Religious Freedom

Do you agree or disagree with the following statement: Religious freedom has grown worse over the past ten years.

% "strongly" + "somewhat" agree

	2012	2015
All adults	33	41
Evangelicals	60	77
Practicing Christians	44	52
Other faiths	19	32
No faith	23	32

Source: Barna OmniPoll, August 2015, N = 1,000
Barna OmniPoll, December 2012, N = 1,008

There is also widespread agreement with the statement "The government has gone too far in limiting the freedoms of Christians." Two-thirds of adherents to faiths other than Christianity and nearly half of those with no faith say they agree.

That day in the Oval Office, we were there to remind the president of his earliest predecessors' commitment to protect a person's freedom of conscience as a sacred human right. A few days prior I had drafted a letter to the president. Cosigning was a group of twelve diverse Christian leaders, people who had been friendly to Mr. Obama, enjoying Easter breakfasts in the East Wing or providing counsel on domestic issues involving people of faith. We didn't send the letter to score political points or to please a constituency; no one who was involved thought that way. Our simple, single goal was to do the small thing we could do: use our meager influence to make sure good faith Americans would continue to enjoy First Amendment freedoms.

> *Dear President Obama,*
>
> *In light of your personal endorsement of the legalization of same-sex marriage, we, as Christian leaders, appeal to you to guide this moment toward respect and civility lest our public square further descend into divisiveness and hatred.*
>
> *Our purpose is not to debate the merits of your opinion on same-sex marriage because we simply disagree. Rather, we ask you to preempt the divisions and bitter wrangling, both political and legal, which are sure to follow. We believe that your leadership will make a decisive difference and that you can lead Americans to be respectful and to find ways to live with one another despite our greatest differences. The genius of the American Founders was in their ability to enable our people to live together notwithstanding their deep religious divisions—ones that parallel our debate about gay marriage. Americans have enjoyed the freedom to promote and live by their moral and religious beliefs—in private as well as public settings, individually and in institutions— without being forced to conform to the latest, evolving moral consensus. But now we are in a moment of peril when these arrangements of mutual respect are at risk.*

After clarifying a few of our concerns and reiterating our commitment to work alongside the president to mitigate rising tensions in the days ahead, we appealed to his unique opportunity to calm the storm:

Mr. President, the nation needs your leadership in making a very strong statement against the swelling trend to label people and institutions that remain committed to historic marriage as being hateful, homophobic, and bigoted. To be sure, some religious people may simply be bigoted. Yet, bigotry is surely not the motive of most who stand for historic marriage and sexual purity. Your own previous views did not suddenly become homophobic just because your opinion changed. Help us elevate this dialogue.

Please speak consistently about the tone of the dialogue when you talk about gay rights and same-sex marriage. Share your disappointment about the extremists on both sides of the divide that would use fear and hate to drive a wedge between Americans. Empower civilized discourse around matters of gay rights and religious rights, and specifically call out those who would treat this as a zero-sum game.

A couple of days after the letter was delivered, I received a call from the White House. "The president would like to meet with you and a few other signatories to discuss this issue. Can you make it next Friday?"

Gulp. "Of course."

So now Pastor Tim Keller, myself, and a couple of others found ourselves sitting (without tea or coffee) with the president, ready to make a personal plea for his leadership in the coming days.

I'd be lying if I didn't acknowledge my trepidation. I didn't want to say the wrong thing and ruin our opportunity. Yet I had a still, quiet assurance that the words would come, that we would say what needed to be said. Instead of thinking I'd somehow worked my way into the Oval Office, I knew that God had appointed this time in this place for his purposes.

Good faith doesn't mean memorizing a script but cultivating a quiet dependence on the God of the universe to meet you in the difficult conversations he brings your way.

I opened the meeting by thanking President Obama for inviting this discussion, and then I jumped right in. Reaffirming the contents of our letter, I explained that we were not there to discuss his theological position on gay marriage but rather to talk about the incredible opportunity he had to lead our country through a conflicted, divisive moment.

I paused to catch my breath, and he nodded to indicate I should go on. I continued, acknowledging his unique opportunity to lead. With the ear of the LGBT community and as a Democrat, like no Republican president could do, the president had a rare opportunity to bring both sides of the gay marriage debate together—toward true tolerance.

The stakes were high. If he didn't lead, the days ahead could get ugly.

Fake Tolerance

We hear the word *tolerance* and nod. Yes, tolerance. Duh, tolerance. Of course, tolerance. We all want tolerance. Who wouldn't? Tolerance is a good thing, right? Yes, except that the meaning of the word has become obscured.

True tolerance is an ability to acknowledge and permit other people's views. To put up with opinions with which you don't agree. To live with ideas and people you find appalling. True tolerance—some call it "principled pluralism"[2]—is a fundamental feature of a truly free society.

But a new definition of tolerance, let's call it "fake tolerance," has emerged over the last decade. It goes something like this: "We will tolerate you as long as your opinion falls within the range of what we deem acceptable." Diverge from society's groupthink on any number of issues, and you are a bigot—or an extremist. In the name of tolerance, fake tolerance is a terrible and ironic counterfeit.

Comedian Bill Maher chastised people who practice *true* tolerance when he quipped that they are "so tolerant, they [tolerate] intolerance."[3]

But, that's the point. Tolerating intolerance is a feature, not a bug, of principled pluralism.

Thanks to fake tolerance, we aren't becoming a "more united" States. If anything, we are more divided than ever. And Americans feel the pressure. A *majority* of adults feel their values and beliefs put them in the *minority* among their fellow citizens. That's right. *More than half of Americans say they feel out of step with the prevailing values of America.* What does this tell us? Everyone feels alienated when those who practice true tolerance shrink into an ever-smaller minority.

Cultural alienation isn't a problem only for Christians. In fact, our data suggest that non-Christians are more likely than non-practicing or nominal Christians to feel outside the American norm. It's the challenge of modern life. The ideological media echo chamber, which specializes in fake tolerance, invites us to become further divided, even tribal. And many of us offer little resistance. It's so much easier to spend time only with those who believe, think, talk, and vote like us.

No wonder division and divisiveness are the order of the day, even as our world is more connected than ever.

Former president Bill Clinton recently remarked, "You know, Americans have come so far. . . . We're less racist. We're less sexist. We're less homophobic than we used to be. We only have one remaining bigotry. We don't want to be around anybody who disagrees with us."[4] Whatever your opinion of him, on this, President Clinton is right on the money.

But hanging around people who disagree with us is exactly what God calls us to do. He calls us to engage with real people, and especially with those who see things differently.

In fact, true tolerance isn't a high enough standard for Christians. To tolerate—to put up with someone—isn't exactly praiseworthy. It should be the lowest bar for a good faith Christian. We are called by Jesus to *love*, not to tolerate. We are called to go far beyond the cultural standard. Our Lord commands us to love our neighbor, even when we vehemently disagree with them. And not only our neighbor. We must also love our enemy. Our physical enemy, our ideological enemy, even the enemy who threatens our life should be the object of our sincere goodwill and godly affection.

When your neighbor despises you—love.

When your enemy attacks you—love.

When a Facebook comment gets under your skin—love. (Yes, even on Facebook—love.)

When a fellow Christian has a different theological perspective than you—love.

There are no excuses or exceptions. If we faithfully live the countercultural life Jesus calls us to, we'll endure uncomfortable situations, lose a few arguments, be embarrassed when we're backed into a corner. And always, in everything, we will love.

Religious Intolerance

An increasing number of Americans aren't sure they should have to acknowledge and permit the historic beliefs of Christianity. With antireligious sentiment strong and a growing divide on what it means to be moral, fake tolerance is on the upswing. For Christians, what does it mean to participate in public life where fake tolerance is applauded and true tolerance is disparaged?

That day in the Oval Office, we offered a specific example of how this is playing out.

I asked if the president was familiar with the Catholic Charities of Boston case. It's a bellwether of this environment. They were forced to shut down their long-standing and well-regarded adoption agency because they couldn't, in good conscience, comply with new state standards that require all agencies to place children into same-sex families. Although many other agencies in the Boston area are happy to serve same-sex couples, Catholic Charities was not exempted from the regulations. They made the difficult decision to shut down operations rather than violate their beliefs about what makes the best family for an orphaned child.[5] Whether or not you agree with their theology and values, less good—not more—is being done for children today because of a law that infringes on religious freedom.

I recall the president shaking his head and expressing dismay that fewer children in need were being cared for. However, he didn't seem very worked up about the threat we perceived to religious freedom. Attempting to allay our concerns, he said, "People of faith will always be free to practice their faith in their churches, mosques, and synagogues."

I think he hoped his response would appease us. It did not. In fact, it had the opposite effect. The president had merely affirmed the most limited interpretation of religious freedom—the same version practiced in communist China.[6] In other words, "Keep it under your own roof and everything will be fine."

Members of our group glanced at each other in a bit of disbelief. Either we weren't persuasive enough or the president was missing the point.

One of his predecessors, founding father James Madison, once wrote, "The Religion then of every man must be left to the conviction and conscience of every man; and *it is the right of every man to exercise it as these may dictate.* This right is in its nature an unalienable right."[7]

The United States of America was the first nation to enshrine religious freedom into law. The freedom to practice a faith different from the country's leader, to associate with others who share our convictions, to fund efforts that align with our beliefs about human flourishing, and not to participate in practices that violate our conscience are fundamental, inalienable rights. These are bedrock American ideas, adopted as the law of the land less than ten years after the Revolutionary War was won. The freedoms spelled out in the First Amendment protect the God-given right of every human being to live by his or her own conscience and prevent government coercion to do otherwise.

Soldiering on in a conversation that had just become even more difficult, Tim Keller pointed out that faiths with a high view of scriptural authority—evangelical and Pentecostal Christianity, traditional Catholicism and Anglicanism, Orthodox Judaism and Islam—are growing around the world. And not just elsewhere, Tim said—even in his hometown, New York City, where he had served in ministry for thirty years. Millions of people in America define themselves as "people of the Book," and asking them to disregard one part of their authoritative text is to demand they abandon the very basis for how they live their lives.

Just a few years earlier, we reminded him, then-senator Obama had made a compelling argument in his presidential campaign for religious convictions in the public square. In his "Call to Renewal" address, he recognized the unique contribution people of faith make to public life and even scolded secularists who hoped to limit the public exercise of their convictions:

> Secularists are wrong when they ask believers to leave their religion at the door before entering into the public square. Frederick Douglass, Abraham Lincoln, William Jennings Bryan, Dorothy Day, Martin Luther King—indeed, the majority of great reformers in American history—were not only motivated by faith but repeatedly used religious language to argue for their cause. So to say that men and women should not inject their "personal morality" into public policy debates is a practical absurdity. Our law is by definition a codification of morality, much of it grounded in the Judeo-Christian tradition.[8]

Two decades earlier he had gotten his first community-organizing job on the south side of Chicago because of the Catholic Church's commitment to social action in the public square.[9] The president knew firsthand the value of public faith.

We reminded President Obama of his own words and work, both of which had contributed to his rise to leadership. At a moment when so much was at stake, we suggested, this was an opportunity for the president to lead the way. He could color the imaginations of the American people so they could see that differences make us better. He could help to make public space for vastly different, deeply held beliefs to coexist in peace.

If America can't figure it out, who will?[10]

As religious conflicts spiral out of control around the globe and true extremists win converts and the news cycle, we must find a way.

A Potluck, Not a Melting Pot

Western democracies are becoming more diverse, not less. As this trend continues, many leaders see that traditional secularism, which insists religion has no place in the public square, is a dead end. There are undeniable historical reasons—mainly post-Reformation political-religious conflicts that lasted for hundreds of years and cost hundreds of thousands of lives—that traditional secularism arose in the West. Secularism separated church and state, ultimately becoming the referee that decides when and where faith can play a role in public life.[11] And taken to an extreme, it ultimately leads to fake tolerance of the Bill Maher variety.

Secularism pays lip service to diversity but has narrow bandwidth for real differences. It prefers the melting pot metaphor for civil society, where our differences melt away and we all become the same. Anything *not* the same is, in the name of tolerance, skimmed off the top and thrown out. In this climate, those who dissent are evil and must be neutralized.

The time has come, we urged the president, for secularism to step aside in favor of "confident pluralism."[12] This is the way forward not just for America and the West but for the world.

Confident pluralists—or principled pluralists, as some prefer—like to think of civil society not as a melting pot but as a potluck: everybody brings their best dish to share, and nobody goes home hungry. No one is forced to eat tuna casserole or green bean salad, but neither are those dishes taken off the buffet to appease those who don't like them.

In a confidently pluralist society, people of good faith do not insist that those who don't share our values be legally compelled to live by them—to eat our green bean salad. That's fake tolerance. But neither should we be compelled by force of law to eat someone else's tuna casserole.

Confident pluralism requires that good faith Christians concern ourselves with defending *everyone's* liberty. This may feel uncomfortable at first for those who are used to Christianity holding a privileged place in American society. But pluralism and, more importantly, Christ's command to love our neighbors oblige us to defend the rights of all citizens to live by their conscience—in and out of the public square.

Yes, this means vigorously defending the rights of our Muslim neighbors to practice faith beyond the neighborhood mosque and of our gay neighbors to publicly express pride in their identity.

* * *

It would be great to report that the meeting with President Obama ended with his declaration of an unwavering commitment to promote confident pluralism as the way forward for US civil society. But, sadly, he did not make such a pledge.

Just a few months later, in the run-up to his second inauguration, the president missed a significant opportunity to model pluralism and true tolerance. Louie Giglio, an evangelical pastor in Atlanta, was initially asked to offer the benediction for the inaugural ceremony. When video surfaced of a twenty-year-old sermon in which Giglio preached on homosexuality and gay marriage, the outcry from LGBT rights groups was deafening.

Rather than insisting Pastor Giglio should bring his green bean salad to the inauguration potluck, President Obama's inaugural committee allowed him to withdraw. (According to some accounts, they may have pressured him to do so.)

The president did not violate Giglio's rights, as some Christians argued at the time—but what a missed opportunity! Can you imagine the impact if President Obama had issued a statement like this?

> I understand the LGBT community's anger at the comments made by Pastor Giglio. In fact, I agree with you—and I do not endorse Pastor Giglio's position or point of view. But that's all the more reason for his participation in the inauguration ceremony. In America, you don't have to agree with everyone else in order to have a place in the public square. You don't even have to agree with the president. Pastor Giglio and his church's work to end human trafficking contributes to the common good in America and around the world. And while I don't agree with his views on sexual orientation and gay rights, I welcome his involvement in the inauguration and in the social fabric of a truly diverse United States.

Unfortunately, such a statement never saw the light of day. As meaningful as our meeting and correspondence with the president had felt going in, I came away from the experience more confident than ever that politics cannot truly solve these problems. The ideas are too embedded at street level to be dislodged by a good speech or a new law. Solving these problems is up to good faith Christians, starting with how we engage our neighbors with whom we disagree.

8

ASSIMILATE OR ACCOMMODATE

Good faith Christians live
their convictions and stand
out from the crowd.

"Mom, Alex ran up to me at the end of school and said a rumor is going around fifth grade that I don't like gay people," said Pierce, Gabe's son.

Needing more information about this latest chapter of public school life in New York City, Rebekah said, "What happened?"

"During last period, Alisha told me that she had a crush on another girl in our class. I was like, 'That's not good. That's wrong.'"

"Really? And what did she say?"

"She was like, 'Why don't you like gay people?' So I told her, 'I never said that, but I think it's against God's laws.'"

Uh-oh, Rebekah thought. "You really said that? Out loud?"

Concerned, Rebekah texted me: You have to call me immediately. Pierce just told a kid at school she shouldn't be gay.

Offended without Warning

Bless his heart. Most kids haven't finished boarding the politically correct train by age ten, and, without meaning to, Pierce had committed one of our culture's cardinal sins. Remember that second principle of the new moral code, which 89 percent of Americans espouse?

Thou shalt not criticize another person's life choices or behavior.

Our public square is rapidly devolving into a place where sharing opinions, especially those that make another person uncomfortable, is off limits. "See something, say something" might work for Homeland Security, but don't try it with a friend. The new social mantra is "See something, keep your trap shut."

But avoiding the risk of offending someone or hurting another person's feelings keeps conversations sterile and impoverished. Don't get us wrong; sensitivity to others is a good and godly thing. But when risk avoidance prevents honest dialogue or a robust discussion of difficult topics, it's time for everyone to do some growing up.

Keeping dissenters quiet isn't just a trend in fifth grade. The drive to create "safe zones" where people are never subjected to opinions or ideas they find offensive can be found everywhere.[1] It's a burgeoning phenomenon on college campuses and in workplaces across America. "It is creating a culture in which everyone must think twice before speaking up, lest they face charges of insensitivity, aggression, or worse."[2]

Many of the same young adults pressing for protection from uncomfortable ideas grew up in protective bubbles that society practically made mandatory. From the banning of peanut butter in school cafeterias to snug-fitting bike helmets, their tender years were safeguarded. Instead of "no pain, no gain," "no gain from pain" would be an apt mantra for the helicopter parents who raised these sensitive souls.

One explanation is the aftermath of the 1999 Columbine school massacre. In the tragedy's wake, "many schools cracked down on bullying, implementing 'zero tolerance' policies. In a variety of ways, children born after 1980—the Millennials—got a consistent message from adults: life is dangerous, but adults will do everything in their power to protect you from harm, not just from strangers but from one another as well."[3]

From "trigger warnings" (alerts that college professors must issue if course content might cause a strong emotional response[4]) to the fight against "micro-aggressions" (unintended or unconscious insults, whether real or perceived, made by nonminorities against minorities), many in the younger generation are emerging into adulthood buffered from harm by safety gates, corner bumpers, and socket covers. Their mental space is so sheltered from cognitive discomfort that, when confronted with an opposing view, they get anxious.

To be fair, Millennials didn't choose to be overprotected; they're the losers of their parents' game. Because protecting people from ideas they'd rather not hear is not only laughable but also ultimately harmful to society. Religious liberty and freedom of speech are rights that can only be put to the test at the distressing intersection of differing ideas. If we run away from that crossroads, these freedoms are simply hypothetical.

Former New York City mayor Michael Bloomberg confronted what some have called the "idea police" at Harvard University, and he did it on their own turf. Many people were shocked when, during his 2014 commencement speech, he rebuked political liberals for repressing conservative ideas:

> In the 2012 presidential race, 96 percent of all campaign contributions from Ivy League faculty and employees went to Barack Obama. That statistic . . . should give us pause. . . . When 96 percent of faculty donors prefer one candidate to another, you have to wonder whether students are being exposed to the diversity of views that a university should offer. Diversity of gender, ethnicity, and orientation is important. But a university cannot be great if its faculty is politically homogenous.[5]

Bloomberg was calling for ideas to clash. He understood that the best ideas win in the end and we need not fear beliefs we disagree with. The truth will prevail. Besides, if our beliefs are never subjected to close examination and rigorous argument, how can we feel the confidence that comes with knowing they are true?

Many twentysomethings are naïve to the real ideological conflicts that older generations, for the most part, assume. Instead of a black-and-white world, they navigate personal disagreements and public engagement in the gray. To cope with all that ambiguity, they digest handpicked comments from social media "friends" and "followers" and interact only with those whom they "like" and with those who "like" them. Tone and wit, not logic, win debates. They live in mental solitary confinement—an echo chamber without a door. No ideas get in or out. It's a safe zone where you can hear yourself talk and feel affirmed when your echo agrees with you.

If you want to be accepted in social settings, the new dogma preaches, hold your tongue or dole out sincere-sounding compliments. Anything else may get you bounced.

I remember fifteen years ago when my coauthor, David, broke the rules. He had noticed that my communication style and manner of leadership, at the ripe old age of twenty-six, were off-putting to my peers. I had no idea. It was a complete blind spot. One day, instead of buttoning his lip or shining me on, he pulled me aside and told me what he was seeing. I was taken aback and embarrassed but then immediately thankful that he cared enough to confront me about a behavior that was unbecoming of the leader I felt called to be.

Some of our most significant learning moments come when a person is bold enough to tell us what we need to hear. As Proverbs 27:6 says, "Wounds from a friend can be trusted" (NIV). It doesn't mean we always like, agree with, or want to hear it. But the freedom to engage our friends at a deeper level of honesty leads to more real and refreshing relationships. Listen—really listen—to opinions you oppose. By making room for disagreement, you make space for friendship.

Not everyone seeks out this kind of challenge, and many may even want to avoid it. But their relationships are poorer for it. As marriage counselors Les and Leslie Parrot say, conflict leads to intimacy.[6] Most of us avoid conflict, thinking life is easier without it. Yet our richest friendships and personal growth opportunities come when we step into the uncomfortable space of conflict, not when we evade it.

Assimilate or Accommodate?

Following Jesus radically redefines the ideas by which good faith Christians live. Our relationship with our Creator is reflected in our words and actions. Our faith demands that we adopt a way of life that honors our King.

In some cases, we have to get weird. This isn't easy. Who wants to be the odd man out, right?

Demonstrating allegiance to King Jesus creates uneasy moments, and we need not seek them out. Merely by faithfully following Christ, we will stand in opposition to a culture that demands our fidelity. As Peter declares in Acts 5:29, "We must obey God rather than human beings!" (NIV). It seems sometimes that it might be easier to go along and get along. But deep in our bones we know that following Jesus requires more.

We have choices to make.

Will we assimilate or accommodate?

Assimilation means embracing the claims, concerns, and commitments of our dominant culture. This is the path of least resistance and will elicit the fewest questions. You will fit right in with the status quo—no hard questions to answer or awkward moments to navigate. Like the disciple Peter, you may be afraid to acknowledge Jesus and the truth that is within you. In the short-term, it may *feel* wise and socially expedient to avoid the difficult conversations.

Accommodation means you choose a countercultural way. Your life stands out as odd and curious, tethered to a different set of truths. This puts you at odds with culture's conventional wisdom. You are confident enough, however, to live alongside those with whom you disagree. For good faith Christians, accommodating those we oppose is critical to maintaining a faithful Christian witness. We must support the right of every person to live by his or her conscience. This means finding ways to accommodate one another even when—no, *especially* when—we hold an opposing view.

With an accommodation viewpoint, we don't seek out conflict. But when the commitments and claims we've made diverge from those of the majority culture, we don't hesitate to stand out.

The Old Testament book of Daniel provides a picture of standing in humble opposition. According to Daniel 3, the Judean exiles Shadrach, Meshach, and Abednego had become provincial leaders in Babylon, a nation that had set itself against the things of God. Somehow, even in exile, they found a way to accommodate this pagan culture without assimilating into it.

But when they were instructed to bow down to the golden image of King Nebuchadnezzar, they stood in boldness—together.

Their non-Jewish peers reported them to the king: "There are some Jews—Shadrach, Meshach, and Abednego—whom you have put in charge of the province of Babylon. They pay no attention to you, Your Majesty. They refuse to serve your gods and do not worship the gold statue you have set up" (Dan. 3:12).

These friends lived under a different set of assumptions about the world they inhabited than the surrounding culture, and their actions showed it. Their lives stood in contrast to those of their peers. The social pressure to assimilate was no match for their faithfulness. They said no.

And their boldness changed the future for their people in exile.

When King Nebuchadnezzar ordered the three Hebrews thrown into a white-hot furnace to die for their treason, he saw a fourth figure beside them in the flames. He cried out:

Praise to the God of Shadrach, Meshach, and Abednego! He sent his angel to rescue his servants who trusted in him. They defied the king's command and were willing to die rather than serve or worship any god except their own God. Therefore, I make this decree: If any people, whatever their race or nation or language, speak a word against the God of Shadrach, Meshach, and Abednego, they will be torn limb from limb, and their houses will be turned into heaps of rubble. There is no other god who can rescue like this! (Dan. 3:28–29).

The king not only accommodated their view but also protected them from others who would not be so accommodating. Obviously, we are not advocating that those who disagree should be cut to pieces—we're in favor of confident pluralism, after all, not barbarism. But Shadrach, Meshach, and Abednego show us the undeniable power of a small group standing for what they believe.

Good faith Christians can sustain a similar humble opposition only if we are prepared and in community. It really can feel like social suicide to adhere to biblical ideas that contradict the ideas our world easily embraces. But we must not grow weary in doing well.

In the "church of culture," the greatest sin you can commit is saying someone else is wrong. No matter how nicely you disagree, it is a real possibility that you could be thrown into the proverbial furnace reserved for social outcasts and cultural traitors. The *fact* that you disagree is enough to convict you, as Pierce found out at school. One-third of Americans say that anyone who believes same-sex relationships are wrong is intolerant. We're not talking about bullying gay kids or evicting a lesbian couple from their apartment—just believing that God's intention for sexuality does not include gay sex.

Being faithful often demands that we express ideas that conflict with the majority culture's claims, concerns, and commitments. What Christians believe about sin, human purpose, identity, and ultimate meaning is at odds with the beliefs of many others. But we can't stay quiet.

* * *

After my plane touched down in Dallas, I got Rebekah's text message.

From the tarmac, I called to get the story. Rebekah gave me a summary, and then she put Pierce on the phone.

"Pierce, what happened?"

Sheepish, Pierce told me his story. "I just know it's not right. In the moment, the words just came out. I'm sorry, Dad."

"Oh, son, don't be sorry. You lived out what you believe, and that's all I can ask for."

After more encouragement, I hung up. But I knew I needed to take it further. So I sat down and wrote a letter to Pierce not only to affirm him but also to coach him through what could be a really tough day at school the next day. It read:

Pierce,

Son, I'm so very proud of you.

FIRST. Today you showed conviction and boldness to state your opinion on how God uniquely designed boys and girls differently. You can't expect that all the other kids will feel the same way. In fact, many of them have been told by their parents that boys liking boys and girls liking girls is okay, even to be celebrated. When you say, "Being gay is wrong," they are very offended because they've been taught to believe anyone who thinks being gay is wrong is a bad person. Remember how we've talked about this world being upside down? What's right is often thought to be wrong. What's wrong is made to seem right. This is a perfect example of that happening. It's okay though. Part of being a Christian is recognizing that we live by different rules than many other people around us. We trust God's words in the Bible and the life of Jesus even if they don't make sense to others.

Now, when you hear people say their opinions—even if you disagree with them—you must always respect them. Jesus says that the first and greatest commandment is "to love God with all your heart" and the second is "to love thy neighbor as thyself." You scored a 100 percent on the first commandment and maybe a 75 percent on the second. Which brings me to the next important point.

SECOND. As a Christian, showing love to all people, even if you disagree with their opinion, is critical for you, Pierce. Loving your neighbor means being a good friend even when they say something with which you disagree. Otherwise they will think you don't care about them or that you think you are better than them.

TOMORROW, when you go to school, friends may approach you. If someone says to you, "Why don't you like gay people, Pierce?" You could respond by sharing your heart the way you did with me tonight.

"I never said I don't like gay people. I love all people. I *believe God made our world so that boys would like girls and girls would like boys. I know you may disagree, and I respect that. But that is my honest opinion."*

Pierce, be prepared that not only students but even teach-ers may disagree with you. And that's okay. Jesus tells us that people who don't know him will be confused about what is good. You need to understand this is an example of a spiritual battle you are facing. It requires courage to follow Jesus in a culture that does not. You can trust that God's Word is true.

I wish I could be with you and give you a huge hug right now. Instead, I'll pray courage for you tonight as you drift off to sleep. God is with you. He loves you and all your friends at school so much. Sometimes it feels lonely to stand up for what you believe, but you are not alone.

I love you.

Dad

Accommodating other views creates difficult conversations. But speaking with love and grace, holding to our convictions, and living counterculturally will go a long way toward seeing truth prevail—even when our views don't align with everyone else's.

Faithfulness is not easy. Traveling this new landscape will require an unshakable commitment to knowing how the world and human beings were designed to operate. But perhaps even more important, it will require an unshakable commitment to love. Love that helps our families navigate the many difficult conversations that lie ahead, and love that speaks and acts with respect for those with whom we disagree.

9

AFTER THE REVOLUTION

Good faith Christians understand the relational consequences of sexual freedom and offer a better way.

I struck up a conversation with my row companion on a recent flight from Washington, DC, to Nashville. After catching a glimpse of the manuscript for this book, she was curious about my work. I did my best to explain that we are describing how good faith intersects the world as we experience it, that no issue is off the table, and that the best of faith applies to all of life. Then she asked, as if to stump me, "What should I say to my sixteen-year-old daughter about hookups? All her friends are so casual about them, but they're shocking to me!"

Taken aback, and knowing (hoping) I have a few more years before I have to engage as a parent on that question, I paused to gather my thoughts. Stalling, I asked, "What's your daughter like? Where does she go to school?"

"Rachel goes to a private school. She's very focused on academics. She's outgoing and social, and her highest priority is going to a great college. Most of her friends have the same goal . . . they see getting into an Ivy League school as their ticket to a great future. Everything else is secondary, including boyfriends."

Recalling Donna Freitas's book *The End of Sex*,[1] I said, "Your daughter's not alone. So many kids in college think it's a normal expectation to hook up. But she's facing pressure to do it at just sixteen years old?"

"Oh yeah! The other night Rachel was at a party with her friends, and three boys texted her to see if she wanted to go into a back room and hook up."

"What did she do?"

"She told them no! But plenty of other girls didn't."

* * *

To anyone paying attention, it's obvious that human relationships are bearing the brunt of the new moral code's repercussions. When virtue is irrelevant and traditional morality is extreme, our children pay the price for a relational world with no boundaries.

Rachel's experience mirrors that of many teenagers and twentysomethings these days. The modern hookup is nearly as casual as going for coffee with a friend was back when we were in college. In her book, Freitas details the incredible pressure on young adults to engage in casual sex with friends or acquaintances. Romantic relationships are an unwanted complication, the thinking goes, but sexual needs must be satisfied. Hookups are the solution, and anyone who doesn't participate in them is just weird.

There are even rules to govern the madness. Rachel's mom explained, "You don't hook up with the same person two weekends in a row. If you hook up with someone this weekend, you take off the next two or you might start to have feelings."

Intuitively, kids know sex is meant for a special relationship. But sexualizing friendships is the new normal. More than half of Millennials agree that "hooking up, or having occasional sex with a friend or acquaintance, is a low-risk way to meet sexual needs." They are twice as likely as Boomers and Elders to agree with the statement.

But casual sex wrecks friendships. For all the momentary fun and exhilaration an afternoon delight may bring, jealousies, awkwardness, and confusion are the ultimate result. When two friends are caught up in the moment—following impulsive lust or just a longing to be held—their friendship faces almost certain ruin.

The longer the idea of hooking up is socially acceptable (and even encouraged) for adults, the more normal it seems to younger and younger teens. Our children are being trained to avoid healthy, intimate relationships at all costs. As we have argued, one of society's highest priorities is individual pleasure—the right to do whatever you please—with no boundaries, no rules. Relationships are almost guaranteed to throw a wrench in those plans. Relationships lead to the painful death of self-focused pursuit.

Constant sexual activity removed from deeper connection is a dead-end road. And the fallout of hookups is leading scores of people to ask, "What good is sex if it only leaves a trail of pain, confusion, and broken friendship?"

This question presents good faith Christians a chance to offer a truly redemptive answer. If we don't, many people will settle for an easier question: How can I enjoy the benefits of sex without the trouble of relationships?

Porn Nation

My son Pierce, who is twelve, often borrows my phone to watch basketball highlights, search top ten dunks, or catch the latest NBA game-winning shot. I keep my eyes on his search results to make sure he's seeing only what he ought to see. He's a good kid and I trust him. He's transparent when things go wrong.

Recently, something went wrong. Handing over my phone, he said, "Dad, I was looking up basketball highlights on You-Tube and this came up. I promise I didn't click on it."

His search had come up with much more than basketball highlights. I glanced at his top result: a barely dressed woman dancing to the latest Jay-Z song with basketball highlights somewhere far in the background.

A scantily clad dancer might not, strictly speaking, be categorized as porn, but I still don't want my basketball-loving kid bombarded with images like that when he goes looking for cool dunks. How can a curious kid avoid this kind of temptation?

As an $8 billion business, porn is one of the fastest-growing segments of the entertainment industry. Porn is consumed by more than fifty million Americans.[2] To put the size and scope of the skin business in perspective, the industry's income rivals that of iTunes digital merchandise sales and the US bottled water industry.[3]

These estimates don't even account for ubiquitous free porn available at the click of a mouse or the swipe of a finger. In October 2015, *Playboy*, the iconic porn magazine that introduced the world to the centerfold, announced it would no longer feature fully nude photos. "You're now one click away from every sex act imaginable for free. It's just passé at this juncture," *Playboy*'s chief executive said.[4]

For most young people, porn is just a normal part of adolescence, like acne or orthodontics. Too much makes you creepy, but a regular dose is okay—healthy even. In a study with Josh McDowell Ministries, we found that, among teens and young adults, using porn squeaks into the top five on a list of possible immoral actions—*and ranks lower than not recycling*. What does America's next generation consider to be immoral?

1. Taking something that belongs to someone else
2. Having a romantic relationship with someone other than a spouse
3. Saying something that isn't true
4. Not recycling
5. Viewing pornographic images

What used to be a niche product—delivered to subscribers by mail in carefully anonymous packaging—has gone mainstream, beamed into every household and smartphone and tablet and laptop with an internet connection, often (thanks to pop-up ads) whether you like it or not. Furthermore, the moral stigma against porn and "soft porn"—sexual images and situations on TV and in movies and video games—is loosening its hold on people. More than half of US teens and adults say, "It really doesn't bother me" to use porn.

Making objects of women or men is no longer something to be ashamed of, and the resulting consumable products are reshaping the imaginations of millions. Our collective culture has been lured into believing that, as long as I'm not hurting anyone, it's okay to indulge myself. Fulfilling my own sexual desire is just easier and less complicated than involving a real-life human being. Porn is even better than hookups at taking relationship out of the equation.

Yet most people also recognize the adverse effects of widespread porn use. Seven out of ten US adults, eight out of ten practicing Christians, and nearly all evangelicals say porn's impact is negative. It affects young people and adults. Everyone is exposed to one extent or another, even if they don't seek it out.

But the biggest losers in our porn-infested culture are not the many millions of porn users, both male and female, whose brains and souls are being warped and calloused. The biggest losers are those we should cherish most: our wives, mothers, sisters, and daughters.

Women Dehumanized

All-out access to sex is not an equal opportunity. Women do the lion's share of the work, as airport magazine racks and roadside billboards will attest. Female bodies are the focus of our culture's sexual obsession. Eight out of ten US adults and nine out of ten practicing Christians agree that our culture objectifies women's bodies.

Look no further than the hack of AshleyMadison.com for a cautionary tale about the foolishness of objectification. Millions of users, the vast majority of them men, were exposed for pursuing "discreet" sexual encounters with married women—who were actually, the scandal revealed, computer-generated "engager bots," little bits of messaging software designed to make men feel like they were engaging with a flesh-and-blood woman. Desiring a no-strings-attached rendezvous, more than thirty-seven million men were swindled.[5]

Society's dominant message about women is clear: women exist for men's pleasure.

> [It is] primarily through the bodies of girls and women that this culture's sexual expression takes place. And it is largely the bodies and lives of girls and women that suffer the consequences through their vulnerability to unwanted pregnancy, greater susceptibility to venereal disease, pressure to look and act like a porn star, and more frequent victimization by sexual assault, rape and sexual harassment.[6]

Viewing another human being as an object erases the image of God. It is not only a sin against that person but also a sin against that person's Creator. Human beings are body, mind, and soul. Emphasizing only one aspect *de*humanizes. Dehumanization is what our culture's sexual obsession does to women.

Recovering Intimacy

People today have nearly unlimited access to casual sex via hookups, porn on demand, web cams, sex toys, masturbation, and countless other options that give them a physical high. Access to orgasms is not the problem.

Easy access to casual sex, porn, and images of naked bodies creates a kind of boredom with the whole idea. The majority culture has become robotic in its thinking about what is meant to be a deeply emotional encounter designed by God to take place in a covenant relationship. It's no wonder the gloss is wearing off. Russell Moore, president of the Ethics and Religious Liberty Commission of the Southern Baptist Convention, says, "The church should prepare for the Sexual Revolution's refugees."[7] Instead of intimacy and emotional depth, sex any way you want it leads to anxiety, depression, loneliness, and insecurity. For some, sex is no longer worth the trouble. Anything more than a one-night stand or porn on demand requires a relationship, and the cost of a relationship is simply too high.

The need for good faith is enormous.

Being truly known, loved, and accepted is what we all long for. We are designed to experience deep and lasting communion with others, but our culture corrupts this divinely given desire and turns it into a quest for sexual experience.

This is where good faith has a lot to offer. Not just dos and don'ts and purity laws, which tend to be the church's simplistic answer. We must witness to God's intention for human relationships. We must model it, teach it, and walk alongside those who are relearning it. And our churches must be safe houses for "refugees" to discover intimacy through relationship as God intended.

In fact, we believe Christian community—the household of God—is the only remedy for the relational and sexual sickness that has infected the culture. How we address matters of sex and sexuality must embody love + believe + live. We need to love others well and see them as made in the image of God, even when they screw up and let us down. In terms of belief, we have to articulate a biblical vision of healthy sex and sexuality. And we must be willing to live out our love and belief in community with real people.

God's household offers life after the sexual revolution. But our idea of "family" must expand to make room for everyone who needs healing.

10

MARRIAGE, FAMILY, AND FRIENDSHIPS

Good faith Christians allow
their marriages, families, and
hospitality to benefit others.

The most significant blow to marriage happened almost fifty years ago.

Thanks to conservative icon Ronald Reagan, marriage is, as far as the government is concerned, nothing more than a contract between two adults. In 1969, then-governor Reagan, a divorced and remarried actor turned politician, was the first to sign "no-fault" divorce into state law.

If you don't like the way your relationship is headed, you can dissolve it with the check of a box. It doesn't matter if your kids will be displaced or whether your spouse has kept their covenantal commitments. As far as the government is concerned, you are within your rights to cancel the contract, move on, and let the rest of the family (and society) pick up the pieces.

No harm, no foul.

If you care about marriage—and not just prohibiting gay marriage—you can't ignore this fact of history.

The fallout has wreaked havoc and devastation in the lives of countless children. Millions of teens and young adults—one-third of them—wake up every morning with only one of their biological parents in the house, making them more likely to drop out of school, to have or cause a teen pregnancy, and to divorce as an adult.[1] It's no wonder young adults are getting married later (if they marry at all). As the graph shows, the average age for first marriages in the United States is twenty-nine for men and twenty-seven for women, compared to twenty-two and twenty, respectively, in 1960.

But the more notable trend is how the curve has gotten steeper in recent years. The age increase between 1990 and 2013 (twenty-three years) nearly matches the rise between 1960 and 1990 (thirty years).[2]

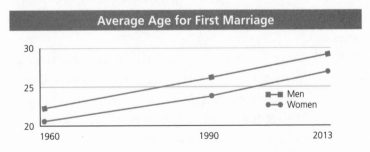

Average Age for First Marriage

Mark Regnerus, a researcher and sociologist at the University of Texas at Austin, once commented during his talk at our Q Conference that the "price of sex is low" and marriage suffers the consequences. As we described in the previous chapter, sex is ubiquitous and easily accessible—and now marriage is no longer the barrier to entry that it once was.

That doesn't mean marriage is entirely off the radar. It's just not a goal for young adulthood as it was fifty years ago. It's on the back burner. Eight out of ten Millennials say, "I want to be married at some point" (82 percent), *but first* . . . "I want to be fully developed as a person" (70 percent), "I want to be financially established" (69 percent), and "I think we should live together" (60 percent).[3] Among the goals twentysomethings want to achieve before they turn thirty, marriage doesn't crack the top five.

What if the church offered a more robust and holistic vision for marriage and family? Instead of personal fulfillment, what if becoming Christlike was the ultimate objective? Marriage, and singleness for that matter, has become more about getting what you want out of life than about discipleship.

Gabe's friend Jay hoped to get married one day but struggled, as so many today do, with finding "the one." The pursuit of the perfect match, one's soul mate, is a modern idea birthed (like so much in our culture) out of the drive for self-fulfillment. For Jay, finding "the one" meant finding a person with a compatible personality, a compelling life story, big dreams for the future, and the desire to have three children. His list was pretty specific.

I told him, "Dude, marriage isn't about you. If you are meant to be married, God will use it to change you." In Christian lingo, we call this "sanctification"—the process God uses to make us more holy, more like Christ. As I explained to Jay, "Sure, marriage may be fulfilling, but more than that it's a significant way God trains us in unconditional love and service. God uses marriage to help you become the person he wants you to be.

"After eighteen years in a marriage," I went on, "I've learned it is a lot like a mirror, reflecting back to me who I really am—whether or not I like what I see. The mirror doesn't lie and neither does my marriage."

This was new information to Jay, even though he had been in Christian environments for years. He had been taught that marriage was the ultimate in relational fulfillment. In many churches, marriage is held up as the best place for deep intimacy, unrivaled by any other relationship. Yet the apostle Paul, in 1 Corinthians 7, provides a different perspective. His call to Christ-followers in Corinth to remain single and not be distracted by the needs of a spouse is quite a contrast to most modern Christian teachings on the pursuit of marriage.

When the Sadducees pressed Jesus on the question of marriage after the resurrection, he responded, "When the dead rise, they will neither marry nor be given in marriage. In this respect they will be like the angels in heaven" (Mark 12:25). This teaching, combined with Paul's instructions, clarifies that singleness is both our origin—our "default setting"—and our ultimate destination. The church, as the bride of Christ, will finally be united with him in the new creation, and each of us will experience the fulfillment and completion we long for in our relationships. But we'll do so in union with our Lord, not in marriage with each other.

Jesus and Paul offer a vision for human relationships that does not rely on marriage but instead prioritizes discipleship.

Good faith Christians recognize that marriage is one avenue of sanctification but certainly not the only way to

Christlikeness. It is one form of intimate relationship but certainly not the only one modeled in the New Testament. Don't get us wrong—marriage is a good thing. But it's not an *ultimate* thing. Where the church has made marriage an idol—elevating it as the one relationship that will bring security, fulfillment, and intimacy—we need to think again.

Marriage as a Community Good

Rob and Lauren have properly weighted their marriage in the balance of their church and community. Having lived in New York City for over a decade, they each had a wonderful group of friends. Once they were engaged, everyone asked, "Where are you going to live?" At first, they assumed they'd get a one-bedroom apartment and start life as an exclusive unit. But when strained finances entered the picture, they pursued a different option: living in a larger apartment with a couple of close friends.

Your first thought might be, *Why would any newly married couple want to live with their friends?* It wasn't their first inclination, but once they embraced the opportunity, their entire understanding of marriage was transformed.

I was catching up with Lauren the other night, and she explained:

> Gabe, our experience has changed how Rob and I think about our marriage. We have this beautiful community of friends, and marriage shouldn't remove us from them. Our marriage shouldn't be just about us but about how we can bring life to others, host dinners, engage in late-night conversations, and be a life-giving part of friendships. Even when we move into our own place one day, we have a completely different picture of how our marriage should be used to benefit others.

Lauren beautifully captured how a holy, outward-facing marriage functions in a larger household of faith. Lauren and Rob don't see their main priority as pairing off from their other relationships. Instead, they see their marriage as a home base for nurturing friendships, welcoming single people, and expanding "family" to include other believers.

We get this idea from Jesus. As the Gospel of Matthew records:

> As Jesus was speaking to the crowd, his mother and brothers stood outside, asking to speak to him. Someone told Jesus, "Your mother and your brothers are standing outside, and they want to speak to you." Jesus asked, "Who is my mother? Who are my brothers?" Then he pointed to his disciples and said, "Look, these are my mother and brothers. Anyone who does the will of my Father in heaven is my brother and sister and mother!" (12:46–50)

Jesus revolutionized what it means to be family. In his vision, family isn't limited to biology; it extends to all those who follow him in doing God's will.

The Missing Ingredient

My transatlantic red-eye brought me into the Netherlands for my first-ever visit to Amsterdam. I had never been there, but my wife's family heritage traces back to the Dutch, and I was excited to see the low country for myself.

In my imagination, the Dutch were traditional people, living the good, old way of life. Pale, sweet-faced women wore wooden clogs (*Klompen*, to be exact) and blue and white dresses and performed a graceful stomp dance, if there is such a thing. Quaint as that picture looked to my mind's eye, it doesn't represent modern Amsterdam—a city notorious for its red-light district and anything-goes morality. In 2001, the Netherlands became the first nation to legalize same-sex marriage. Its trailblazing legalization of abortion, euthanasia, and prostitution paved the way for many other European nations to implement similar laws. Its modern society is a long way from my stereotypes of clogs and stomp dances!

I met with several Christian leaders—mostly church planters and entrepreneurs motivated by faith to advance the gospel in their city—and learned a lot about engaging post-Christian culture. European cultural contexts can help us envision where American life may be headed. In the Netherlands, religion is seen as merely irrelevant tradition. Anyone who takes it too seriously is considered extreme. This has forced the faithful to adopt an almost-forgotten essential of gospel living.

Hospitality.

The church leaders shared stories of how conversations about faith were happening because of hospitality. Whether someone was hosting refugees passing through from the Middle East or inviting a colleague over for dinner, the themes of welcoming, celebrating, and humanizing the stranger came up again and again. In Amsterdam, hospitality is a standout, countercultural idea.

It's nothing new. Actually, it's quite old, confiscated by modern life when hotels, hospitals, and homeless shelters institutionalized hospitality. (We even have a hospitality industry.) But it's a clear biblical priority, even mentioned as a spiritual gift (see 1 Cor. 12). Perhaps because it's so rare in our times, hospitality beautifully expresses God's vision for human relationships.

One way to practice hospitality is to express interest in others. It's easy to talk about yourself. But try asking more questions than you are asked in your conversations. It's a simple but profound truth: people enjoy sharing about themselves, and it helps them feel welcome and special. Difficult conversations can be a little less imposing if we make it our goal to really get to know the other person.

All of this may sound like Relationship 101, but the importance of hospitality caught my attention like a lighthouse on a foggy night. Showering tangible love on those we know—and on those we don't—allows people to experience the love of Jesus in ways they don't see coming. Hospitality is good faith in action. In a culture that emphasizes fast meals, online friendship, and casual hookups, hospitality is a truly countercultural experience. The recipient is left longing for more.

Historically, God's people have been the best—even radical—when it comes to hospitality. "In a number of ancient civilizations, hospitality was viewed as a pillar on which all morality rested. For the people of ancient Israel, understanding themselves as strangers and sojourners, with responsibility to care for vulnerable strangers in their midst, was part of what it meant to be the people of God."[4] Jesus practiced welcome in ways that confounded the religious elites. He ate in the home of a tax collector, fellowshiped with "sinners," and enjoyed long meals with his disciples. He was so good at showing up at parties that he was accused of being a drunk.

Then Paul took it to a new level. In his letters, he introduced the concept of "households," groups of assorted believers in all stages of life pursuing godly living together. As pastor Greg Thompson points out, "Many of us are not used to talking about households. And in Christian theology, while the household includes families, it was never limited to them. It not only included all who call on the name of Jesus, but those who needed to find shelter within them."[5]

If the idea of hospitality feels a bit strange in our current culture, we must remember it is rooted in Christian theology. "The people of God are aliens and strangers whom God has welcomed into the 'household of faith.' In turn, God's people are to 'make room' for the stranger, not only in the community of faith but also in their own personal households."[6]

An Open-Door Policy

Have you ever watched *Duck Dynasty*, the popular reality series set in Louisiana that portrays an extended family's household of relationships? Behind the cameras and scripted storylines, Willie and Korie Robertson beautifully model hospitality.

Recently, the Lyons family visited the Robertsons in West Monroe. Everywhere we turned, we heard another story of generous Christian hospitality. It was almost unbelievable to see the number of lives and families impacted by their commitment to hospitality.

After a hearty crawfish pasta dinner (one of "Chef Willie's" favorites), we savored warm blueberry cobbler in the Robertsons' living room. Leaning back in a recliner with a carb overload, I said to Willie and Korie, "I'm so overwhelmed and refreshed to witness the beautiful way you guys live your lives. I keep meeting people who have one more story of how your family has impacted them. They all feel a part of your family. It's amazing!"

A bit embarrassed, Willie responded, "Gabe, we are just living life, man . . . not doing anything special, just doing what's right. We are blessed."

What I witnessed in those twenty-four hours inspired and convicted me. The web of relationships—family and friends—they have woven is countercultural in the most astonishing, and inviting, way. I encountered three unique relationships in West Monroe that offer a vision of what a modern-day household of faith could look like—even if you don't like crawfish.

First we met Brian, a twenty-six-year-old man who moved to Louisiana several years back to take care of his mom. When he began looking for a job, he had no luck. He had a criminal record, and employers didn't think twice about skipping right past his name. Unfortunately, discrimination against former inmates still gets praise in many communities. But Brian was looking for a fresh start and was willing to take any job.

When Duck Commander, one of Willie's companies, hired him out of hundreds of other applicants, Brian was blown away with gratitude. The Robertsons didn't mind his history because they saw his real potential. And given the opportunity, he did an outstanding job. He grew in his skills and recently became a manager of another of their businesses.

As we talked, Brian said to me, "I love Willie. He saved my life and introduced me to Jesus. I'll never work for anyone else!"

Then there is Rebecca. Her friendship with the Robertsons began her junior year in high school when she was a foreign exchange student from Taiwan who came to live with their family. In time, she was fostered and then naturally folded into their family. Today, at age twenty-seven, she helps run a designer fashion boutique, Duck and Dressing, and is actively pursuing adoption so she can give to someone else what was given to her.

The Robertsons adopted one child at five weeks old—and they just keep on adopting. When Korie recently became aware of a twelve-year-old boy who needed a permanent home, she instantly said, "Yes!" With their oldest son heading off to college, they said, "We have a free room opening up in the house. Let's welcome another family member."

This is how good faith Christians do family: as a household of faith, with an open-door policy.

You may not think you have the capacity, space, or resources to continually expand your household the way the Robertsons do. But each of us can invite a new friend or acquaintance over for dinner, go out of our way to support adoptive families, and invest time in the life of a child, teen, or young adult. You might even consider fostering a child without a permanent home.

Each family has its own unique dynamics, but Christ calls us beyond our fears and desire for comfort to trust him. We can be confident that when we welcome the stranger, we are welcoming Jesus into our midst.

Our world hungers for friendships, marriages, and families. These are wonderful gifts that are deeply needed, but we can offer something even better. Hospitality creates households of faith where every person can belong.

11

LIFE, DEATH, AND DISABILITY

Good faith Christians believe
every human life—in every form,
at every stage—matters.

Soaked in sweat, flying alone on a plane chartered by the Centers for Disease Control, Dr. Kent Brantly didn't know if he would live or die. Less than a year before, motivated by faith, the Brantlys had moved to Monrovia, Liberia, so Kent could serve a medical mission. Little did he or anyone else know that, just five months later, the most deadly and contagious virus to erupt in decades would walk into his clinic.

Now Kent himself had been struck down by the deadly virus he'd been fighting for months in Monrovia: Ebola.

Only weeks before, word of the first case had arrived. Because it was two hundred miles away, Kent and his team weren't too worried—after all, there were many other deadly diseases to be concerned about in West Africa. What were the chances this would become an epidemic? But the warning was enough for the team to prepare. They knew that, if Ebola reached their town, death would come to most who contracted it. The medical team created special facilities, trained on protocols, and stocked up on all the personal protective equipment they could find that might help them fight off the virus.

It didn't take long for their premonitions to come true. As Ebola spread throughout West Africa, Monrovia became ground zero for the epidemic. Kent, knowing the risks, committed to stay and help.

Then his worst nightmare came true. One morning he woke with symptoms and understood that he now faced the same dark path so many other patients before him had walked. At the urging of Samaritan's Purse, the relief organization that had sent Kent to Liberia, the American government intervened and decided to bring him home. He laments to this day that others didn't have the same opportunity and lives with some survivor's guilt after recovering from Ebola in the following months.

Many people have asked Kent if his faith is what healed him from the deadly virus. After sharing how grateful he is to be Ebola-free, his response is always the same: "Actually, it is my faith that's responsible for me getting Ebola in the first place, because it led me to serve the people of Monrovia, Liberia."

This is the way a good faith Christian thinks.

People of good faith risk their comfort, reputation, and even their lives for the lives of others. They not only fight deadly diseases but also defend the value of life along its entire continuum. They give voice to those yet to be born, respect and affirm the dignity of people who are disabled, and ensure life extends until its natural end.

Christians believe that every human life—in all its forms, at every stage—matters.

We are called to protect life as God's good gift to us. Each life is a miracle, bearing witness to God's infinite creativity and faithful intention to bless our world through people created in his image. Jesus had a pretty extreme view of how much we should value life. He taught that we are to love our neighbors, even when doing so could endanger our lives. "There is no greater love than to lay down one's life for one's friends" (John 15:13).

A deep commitment to valuing life is well documented from the second century, when Christians were known to go outside the city gates to rescue unwanted babies and abandoned children.[1] During the deadly plagues in Rome, when doctors and leaders fled to save their own lives, Christians stayed to provide bread and water to the sick.[2]

As a good faith Christian, Dr. Kent Brantly comes from a long tradition of selfless, reckless compassion.

Valuing All of Life

Over the last five decades, the majority of Christian engagement around "life" issues has focused on tightening abortion laws and working to shut down clinics. It's hard to argue with the motivation: more than fifty-four million abortions have been performed in America since the 1973 *Roe v. Wade* Supreme Court decision.[3] Some Christians don't appreciate pro-lifers' noise. They wish antiabortion activists would pipe down and move on to more culturally palatable social issues. Thank God they have not.

David and Jason Benham have faithfully worked on this issue all their lives. Their father, Flip Benham, led Norma McCorvey (better known by the legal pseudonym "Jane Roe," plaintiff in *Roe v. Wade*) to Jesus during their childhood. David and Jason pray on sidewalks outside abortion clinics and, every chance they get, speak up for the unborn in public forums.

The latest innovations in medical technology provide proof of life from the earliest moments in the womb. Groups like Save the Storks offer free ultrasounds in their mobile units, allowing a mom-to-be to see with her own eyes her child's beating heart. Alternative pregnancy support centers, like Avail in Manhattan and Caris Pregnancy Counseling and Resources in Chicago, offer women a *real* choice. In contrast to the options available from groups such as Planned Parenthood (whose own statistics reveal that "choices" are not presented in equal measure[4]), a woman is offered care, counseling, and support throughout her pregnancy and beyond so that, in her early years of motherhood, she is not alone.

In addition, more postabortive women are sharing their stories publicly. The promise of a carefree life rarely pans out. From depression and mental health issues to lasting shame and guilt, women often suffer when they end a life.

Good faith Christians must push back against a culture that views life as disposable. And our value of life must be holistic. We must focus not only on protecting life prior to birth but also on nurturing children after they are born. This means supporting mothers-to-be who are scared, ashamed, and uncertain; churches must come alongside women to help them forge a viable future for their child.

Nurturing children after they are born also means adding to the increasing number of adoptive and foster families in our churches. The growing emphasis on adoption and foster care—and more recently, the concern Christians have expressed about care for refugees—is a bright spot among followers of Jesus in the last decade. We see evidence of this positive trend in our research. Five percent of practicing Christians, compared with 2 percent of all US adults, have adopted children. Three percent of practicing Christians are foster parents, and 31 percent have seriously considered fostering a child. By comparison, 2 percent of all adults are foster parents, and 11 percent have seriously considered fostering a child.[5] We pray these numbers continue to rise in the coming years.

This is the kind of good faith that disarms the culture of death.

Natural Death

David Kuo was a dear friend. It is still hard for me to speak of him in the past tense. His brotherly affection, encouragement, and singular voice still influence me. "Be faithful, you moron. Don't screw this up. God's gifted you, Gabe, and you better keep pressing in," he said in one of our final conversations before his death in 2014. I don't know that I've met a more sincere, bold, and committed follower of Jesus than David. Like all of us, he had his rough spots, but God fashioned a beautiful soul in this multitalented man.

David lived a lot of life after he was given six months to live. He served as a special assistant to President George W.

Bush, wrote a *New York Times* bestselling political memoir, and founded a media start-up. His brain cancer, diagnosed in 2003, was declared incurable, but that didn't stop him. He pursued an aggressive treatment plan, including risky brain surgery, because he was determined to stay in the game. And when the cancer returned, he fought on, undergoing two more brain surgeries over the next ten years.

David's dear wife, Kim, and so many of his friends were thrilled to watch him live long past that first diagnosis. Instead of six months, we enjoyed another decade with him.

David's unexpectedly extended life span not only benefited him but also dramatically enriched the lives of others. First, David and Kim brought new life into the world, giving birth to two beautiful children. Second, as his rhythm of life changed, David found more margin and energy to spend time with a community of Christian leaders who benefited from his wisdom and sober-mindedness. His brushes with death made him fearless, no longer concerned about his reputation. He pressed into our lives and called us out, pushing us to live into all God called us to.

The decade after David was given six months to live was, arguably, his most fruitful.

In society today, the trends point in a troubling direction. According to one recent poll, 69 percent of Americans believe it should be legal for doctors to end a patient's life if the person is terminally ill and requests assistance to die painlessly.[6]

After being diagnosed with brain cancer at the age of twenty-nine and given six months to live, Brittany Maynard launched a campaign called "My Right to Die with Dignity at 29."[7] After selecting a date to end her life, she posted videos to count down the days, advocating for the right to die, not just for herself but for anyone who wants to control the timing of their death.

Millions of people followed Brittany's personal, now public, story.[8] Many Americans were caught off guard. Why would this beautiful young woman forego treatment and prematurely end her life?

As Brittany approached her final three days, she let the world in on her internal struggle. "I still feel good enough and I still have enough joy and I still laugh and smile with my family and friends enough that it doesn't seem like the right time right now."[9] But then she reassured herself, "But it will come, because I feel myself getting sicker. It's happening each week." Can you feel her tension and doubt? In a moment of vulnerability, she seemed to be fighting second thoughts, uncertain if this was the right time to die.

Brittany ended her life on November 1, 2014, with drugs prescribed by her doctor. She became her own arbiter of life and death, believing she knew best when to die.

David Kuo left it up to God. Kim Kuo, his widow, wrote later:

As Pope Francis observes, assisted suicide gives us a "false sense of compassion." Choosing suicide at any point is the same sin Adam and Eve committed in the garden: the pride of wanting to be God, *not simply to serve him*. True compassion is surrounding a terminal patient with love, support, and palliative care. . . . Are we willing to surrender to our Creator the specifics of how and when we die? How much do we actually trust him with our final days?[10]

When we take death into our own hands, we reveal our lack of trust in God. And we reenact the original sin: wanting to be God, in control of our own lives.

It's understandable. Few people want to stare pain in the face and walk forward. We've been culturally conditioned to avoid suffering at all costs. But according to the apostle Paul, suffering is not necessarily something to be avoided (see Rom. 8:16–18). In fact, in suffering we may experience grace that can be found nowhere else.

Good faith Christians like David Kuo trust that death will ultimately be defeated. "For Christ must reign until he humbles all his enemies beneath his feet. And the last enemy to be destroyed is death" (1 Cor. 15:25–26). God promises resurrection in Christ because he is a God of life.

And good faith Christians must be people of life.

The Grace of Disability

I like to tease my wife, Rebekah, about one of her high school accomplishments that few people know about. Not only was she first chair trumpet (the only girl alongside thirteen boys), but she was also the drum major for her high school marching band. You can imagine my thrill when we visited her childhood home early in our marriage and I discovered the National Drum Major Champion trophy. From an early age, Rebekah found significance in achieving.

Both Rebekah and I thrived in performance-based environments. When achievement and recognition were motivators, we responded like Pavlov's dogs. We were good at hitting our goals, making the teams, and winning the championships.

It wasn't long into our marriage that our flawed ways of measuring significance were shattered. We learned that God couldn't care less about performance-based self-worth—and we learned that lesson through our firstborn son, Cade.

I was twenty-six years old when Cade was born with Down syndrome. Children with Down syndrome have one extra chromosome and are often characterized by delayed mental and physical development and a joyful disposition. They have significant potential, but it can take a little longer to develop.

If Rebekah and I were counting on our son's performance to validate our parenting, we were in for a rude awakening.

During the toddler years, we inundated him with eight weekly therapies and wooden contraptions to keep his hips aligned and aid his potential to stand up. We were so determined to help him achieve. But even on the special-needs charts, Cade missed the mark. On basic milestones—crawling, saying his first words, interacting with other children—he fell further and further behind.

It was a shock to discover that, for some things, more practice and mental toughness aren't the answer. When life has always been up and to the right, like a business growth chart, that lesson is almost impossible to learn.

But Rebekah and I often wondered, *What is God trying to teach us?*

Cade would be our teacher. He would help us throw the performance-based measuring stick in the fire.

Children like Cade are a threat to modern societies. Not because his disability *physically* threatens anyone. Rather, because typical people can hide their imperfections but the disabled always have theirs on display, Cade is an in-your-face reminder that aspirations for perfection are flawed and hopeless. People like Cade disrupt and redefine society's definition of human value.

While he does, technically speaking, have a "disability," our family, friends, and community recognize his gifts and unique abilities. On the streets of Manhattan, Cade never met a stranger. Always quick to interrupt a self-consumed soul, he would insist that passersby remove their headphones and speak a hello to his waving hand. In subways, he would crowd onto any inch of plastic seat he could spot, often to the initial dismay of a distracted and defensive passenger. But Cade could sense their temperament and would make every effort to connect. More often than not, they would reciprocate the attention and a beautiful moment would happen.

This is the upside-down way of Jesus that makes a world in which disability is a grace.

The gift of Cade saved my life. My wise therapist told me one day, "Your unconditional acceptance, joy, and love for your son is exactly how your heavenly Father feels about you." His words hit me like a ton of bricks.

There is nothing I can do to earn higher approval. My performances don't impress. My achievements have been for my glory, not yours.

I was embarrassed, ashamed even. And then so relieved. All this wisdom from a teacher whose words you might hardly understand. This is the grace of the disabled among us. They not only enrich our lives but also teach us some of life's most important lessons.

They show us our own insufficiencies.

They teach us how to have joy in any circumstance.

They reshape our definition of perfect.

They alter career paths and require families to work together.

They invite us to engage instead of simply walking by.

They love unconditionally, asking little in return.

In a 2015 episode of The Liturgists podcast on the topic of abortion, musician Michael Gungor, who also has a child with

Down syndrome, told a story about his wife, Lisa, who was at a support meeting for moms with Down kids. The group was meeting in a coffee shop, and a woman who was walking by asked what they were meeting about. When the group leader explained what had brought the moms together, the woman said, "Oh. I thought they just took care of that nowadays."[11]

At its worst, our culture diminishes the value of those who don't immediately appear to "benefit" anyone. Good faith Christians, on the other hand, believe that every human life matters—that *every* human being, no matter his or her number of chromosomes, is indelibly imprinted with God's image and is therefore of infinite worth.

For the first eight years of her life, our daughter, Kennedy, never heard the words "Down syndrome." We didn't try to hide Cade's diagnosis from her, but we wanted her to know and love Cade as a person—not as a "special need" or a "kid with Down's."

The relationship between those two is unbelievably sweet. From her playing teacher for our version of summer school to instructing him in the fine art of ballroom dance, Kennedy brings confidence and joy out of Cade.

We could never have anticipated what a gift Cade would be to us. But I can tell you that not a day goes by that we don't consciously thank God for sending this beautiful boy into our family.

12

RACE AND PREJUDICE

Good faith Christians admit their racial bias, see the image of God in others, and build diverse friendships.

If we get relationships wrong, little else matters.

The Christian God is a relational God. He exists relationally within his Triune self—as Father, Spirit, and Son—but God's actions in the world are also driven by a mission to reconcile his relationship with humanity. He was so intent on this mission that he emptied himself by becoming the "other"—a human being.

We see a similar drawing close to the other in the way Jesus discipled the Twelve. He chose followers and friends with different experiences and lifestyles. Their differences—from fisherman to tax collector, hotheaded to cool and calculating—reflected God's mosaic history of forging unlikely relationships to accomplish his mission.

If you have a few years of life experience under your belt, you know that human relationships are one of the primary places God does his good work of redemption and re-creation, sanctifying us into the people we were created to be. Relationships are the engine of God's transformative work in us. And it is often when those relationships are most difficult, when the differences between us are most profound, that the deepest of God's sanctifying, reconciling work is done.

How good faith Christians engage in relationships says more about the truth of what we believe than all our well-argued apologetics or carefully worded doctrinal statements.

How do we respond to those who live and think differently? Do we see ourselves as better and smarter? Are we open to learning lessons we've never even imagined about our world and ourselves?

Good faith does not prioritize relationship with God over and against relationships with one another. It reveals relationship with God in relationships with others.

I like to be a part of solving problems. Wisdom warns that no one person has an infallible perspective on any situation. Proverbs reminds us, "Where there is no counsel, the people fall; but in the multitude of counselors there is safety" (Prov. 11:14 NKJV). Because I don't have all the answers, I convene others who might. That urge to bring people and ideas is the impetus behind Q. It's common for me to respond to pressing issues in the church or the broader culture by inviting a group of thoughtful people with different points of view and takes on reality into a room to listen to one another and talk about those issues. Some already have relationships with one another, while others embark on new and unlikely friendships. In either case, our guards are let down. We roll up our sleeves and try to find a way through together.

For me, the need to convene in pursuit of wisdom never felt more urgent than in 2014 and 2015, when race once again rose to the surface of our national consciousness. Of course for many it has been a front-and-center reality *for their entire lives*, but in the last few years, many Americans began to understand that the questions of racial reconciliation were not as settled as we imagined.

When Trayvon Martin and then Eric Garner and then Michael Brown and then Tamir Rice and then Freddie Gray were killed, and then protests arose in Ferguson and Baltimore and around the country, I began to see—really *see*—the pain, grief, and righteous anger of African Americans. Like many of my white brothers and sisters, my gut reaction was to point out the importance of obeying the law and cooperating with law enforcement. But as I began to listen also to my black brothers and sisters, it became clear they saw these deaths not as isolated tragedies but as the latest iteration in a long, long history of death.

I realized that, when it came to race in America, I was *way* out of my depth. I felt lost at sea. On many cultural topics, I have at least a working knowledge of the history and issues involved. But on race, there was something going on beyond what I could begin to understand on my own.

So I did the thing I know how to do: I convened.

I made some calls and set a date, and the governor offered the Tennessee Residence as a place where ten black leaders and ten white leaders, all Jesus people down to the core, could get together and talk about what Christians can and should do about the deep and persistent racial divides in the church and the country.

The appointed day came—a beautiful, sun-dappled Nashville morning that seemed to promise peace and reconciliation. I was savoring the winding drive through the neighborhood that surrounds the governor's mansion, admiring the stately, gracious elegance of the historic homes, when suddenly it occurred to me: *some of these properties were once plantations.*

This was followed by a sickening question: Had the governor's mansion—the place I'd invited descendants of slaves to share their stories and offer their wisdom—also been a plantation?[1]

A pit opened up in my stomach. How had this not crossed my mind until this moment? Through the many weeks of planning and preparations, not once had I or anyone who works with me thought to consider the location's history and what it might mean to our honored guests.

I gripped the steering wheel as my hands got clammy, and that's when it dawned on me. *This is what they mean by "white privilege."*

As a white guy in America, I have the luxury of (mostly unconsciously) expecting to belong just about anywhere I want to go. I rarely worry about whether I'll feel like an outsider or whether anyone will be suspicious of my presence or intentions or will question my ability or right to speak my mind, pay for what I want, or succeed on my own merits. Even more fundamentally, I (mostly unconsciously) assume my views and experiences are the universal norm—everyone else is "other." That's why it had not occurred to me that anyone would feel uncomfortable or alienated at the historic governor's residence: *I* didn't feel uncomfortable or alienated, so how could anyone else?

I'm thankful for that drive and the troubling things I discovered about myself. But I'm even more grateful for what I learned that day. Listening to the stories and perspectives of nineteen other leaders changed me. As the day unfolded, their wisdom illuminated some paths forward, not only for the issue of race in America but also for how Christians are called to relate to anyone who is the other.[2]

Honor the Image of God in Each Person

Every human being carries an indelible imprint of God's image (see Gen. 1:27). Nothing else in creation bears this mark. As Lisa Sharon Harper, evangelical and longtime mobilizer for racial and economic justice, says, "It's the thing that actually makes us human." As his image-bearers, we are God's representatives, entrusted with the job of exercising "dominion" (Hebrew *rada*) as stewards of creation. For Lisa, the idea of exercising dominion is inextricably linked to a person's agency—their capacity to *act*.

Many factors can limit a person's agency, but the two most systemic—that limit not just individuals but entire communities or groups of people—are poverty and oppression. When people don't have and can't get the resources they need to provide for themselves and their families, their capacity to act as God's representatives is limited by their needs. Likewise, when people are unjustly burdened by others' unchecked power, their agency is limited by social, legal, and cultural inequity.

Most US adults recognize that the agency of people of color, in particular, is often limited in this way: seven out of ten Americans agree that people of color "are often put at a social disadvantage because of their race."

For Christians, this might translate, "People of color are often limited in their ability to act as God's representatives"—not because they are black or brown but because of the social, legal, and cultural inequities that are the enduring legacy of racial oppression. And yet evangelicals—the vast majority of whom are white[3]—are *more than twice as likely* as the general population to "strongly disagree" that people of color are socially disadvantaged because of race. They are also *twice as likely* to "strongly agree" that "racism is mostly a problem of the past, not the present."

Talk about a blind spot!

These research findings lend weight to Lisa's opening thought on that sunny Nashville morning: "The widest divide in worldview in America is found not between [politically] liberal blacks and [politically] conservative evangelical whites. The widest divide is between black and white evangelicals."[4] Our African American brothers and sisters testify that there are critical ongoing problems with racial inequality in this country, but too many of us do not hear.

We must start to listen—yes, because it's the right thing to do but more importantly because God handcrafts human beings of every hue in his own image to act as stewards over creation. And our society's unholy habits of injustice and inequality degrade and disempower God's image-bearers.

Christians of good faith recognize and honor the image of God even—or especially—in the other. And therefore it's time for us to repent of our (and our forebears') contributions to injustice and inequality, even if those contributions have been unintentional. We must deal with the past and prepare for a more (not less) diverse future.

We should pursue reforms so that our systems—criminal justice, academic, economic—reflect racial equality and fair application of the law. Children should have access to a good education no matter their skin color or zip code. Black men, women, and children should not be arrested, convicted, and imprisoned at higher rates than other ethnicities.

We might differ on the precise mechanisms for meeting these ends, but we must prioritize justice over partisan objectives. We should also reject the use of racial issues to stoke fear and political appeals to racial animus. Our systems and our politics should reflect a biblical understanding of human dignity and equality.

Confront Racial Bias in Ourselves and Each Other

We all have biases. But the ones that should scare us most are those we can't or won't admit. Explicit bias is on display for all to see, but the most destructive prejudices are hidden, packed so far down in our psyche that we don't even know they're there.

Growing up in rural Virginia, I experienced this firsthand. Where I come from, racial differences were underlined for emphasis. A general policy of white superiority reigned over schools, churches, and neighborhoods. There were no-go zones, certain parks and such-and-such streets, where whites knew to stay away. Not because the black community had issued some kind of warning but because whites were afraid. Growing up in that environment, bias is the air you breathe.

Those feelings sink in. And they can take years, decades, or even a lifetime to overcome.

As my friend David Bailey has helped me to understand, these unspoken or even unacknowledged biases are at the root of most racial animus in America today. David, a modern-day peacemaker, defines "implicit racial bias" as the unconscious attitudes or stereotypes related to race that affect our perceptions, actions, and decisions. There may be fewer true racists in post–Civil Rights America, but that doesn't mean racism is dead and gone. Instead, it has a new face: *implicit* racial bias. Our biases are not explicit or deliberate, yet they have enormous power over how we see society overall and individuals who look, speak, and live differently than we do.

David Bailey is part of a community in Richmond, Virginia, called Arrabon that trains people to be multiculturally competent and to form reconciling communities. That day at the governor's mansion in Nashville, he explained implicit racial bias like this: "Gabe is over six feet tall and pretty broad across the shoulders, but he has probably never been referred to or even thought of as a big scary white dude. But 'big scary black dude' just sounds normal. *That's* implicit racial bias."

The only remedy for people of good faith, David says, is for us to intentionally become aware of our unconscious biases with the help of a diverse Christian community.

Those relationships can change everything.

In seventh grade, I met my new best friend, Cedric. We did everything together—from going to church and Awana to climbing around in the woods and playing sports. Cedric's was one of only a few black families in a church made up mostly of whites. They welcomed me into their home without hesitation. And as I look back, my friendship with Cedric was a fresh wind that blew through the stale air of racial bias I had breathed since birth. There were still plenty of unacknowledged assumptions and prejudices, but there is no doubt in my mind that my implicit biases would have been more stubbornly rooted in my heart had it not been for my relationship with Cedric and his family.

The problem for the church is that many (if not most) Christian communities in the United States are homogenous—that is, not diverse at all. And layered atop the problem of most churches' ethnic homogeneity is the popular idea that the "good Christian" thing to do is to practice colorblindness—where we ignore differences altogether. Out of a sincerely good intention to judge others "not by the color of their skin but the content of their character," as Martin Luther King Jr. challenged, white people often make an effort to see everyone the same—at least consciously. But colorblindness does not make space for people to appreciate different social narratives and cultural expressions. It also tends to make white people defensive—as if, by merely acknowledging differences exist, we are racists. And when we're defensive, it's almost impossible for us to be vulnerable and honest enough to become aware of our biases.

It's a vicious cycle, but good faith Christians can escape by building true friendships with believers of other ethnicities who help us confront our unconscious assumptions.

Acknowledge Our Poverty of Friendships

If building true friendships across ethnic and racial divides were easy, everyone would do it. But the truth is that most of us live in a "racialized reality." Our everyday interactions are peopled mostly by those who look, think, and act like us.

Intentionally or not, most of us maintain friendships with people who are ethnically and culturally similar to us. These relationships distort our perception of reality.

Just 17 percent of Americans say it is "completely accurate" that they enjoy spending time with people who are not like themselves. That low number may be one reason many white people were caught off guard—downright shocked might be more accurate—by the intense anger black Americans expressed through the protests in Ferguson, Baltimore, and elsewhere; too few of us spend time outside our own bubble and didn't see it coming.

Chris Heuertz was mentored by Mother Teresa and is an advocate for what he calls "contemplative activism." He believes that the racialization of our daily reality leads to a deep poverty of friendships. In the governor's mansion in Nashville, he challenged us to take a look at the last ten texts and phone calls on our phones. "If you're a twentysomething Protestant black woman or a fiftysomething straight white man, most of the calls or texts you send and receive are to and from people who look like you, think like you, live like you, worship like you." This lack of what Chris calls "textured diversity" keeps us poor in friendship and keeps us believing there is an *us and them* rather than a *we*.

Mother Teresa used to say, "We need the poor more than the poor need us." Chris wrestled for many years to understand what she meant by those words. He now believes that it's only through relationships with the other—the poor, the gay, the Catholic or charismatic, the black or white or brown—that we can become the *we* Christ intends the church to be. We need "them" if we want to be a signpost pointing to the new creation. When we form and cultivate friendships with the other, the *we* of the church becomes a tangible, visible sign of the kingdom of God.

Where should good faith Christians start?

Perhaps for you it will begin by pursuing a friendship with someone of a different ethnicity. Others might join a minority-led faith community for worship. Read writers and thinkers who do not share your cultural background; loving the other means actively trying to excavate, understand, and wrestle with their personal and community narratives. To do this you may need help; seek a mentor of a different color who can lead and coach you.

We believe pastors and other church leaders have a special responsibility to pursue racial reconciliation and church unity—and a majority of Americans back us up. Three-quarters of US adults agree that "Christian churches play an important role in racial reconciliation." Especially if you are a white leader, we urge you to start listening to your fellow leaders who are also people of color. Consider inviting a local nonwhite pastor to your home or out for a meal. Explore the possibility of partnering in ministry with churches in your community that have a different ethnic majority than your church (and don't assume you'll take the lead). Share your pulpit with clergy from a different cultural background. Organize a regular "worship swap" with another church that uses a different style of music. Bring together ethnically diverse church leaders and congregations for an annual or even quarterly joint service.

Beyond that, consider how you can partner with minority church leaders to create safe spaces for grace-filled conversations where learning, understanding, and healing can happen. As Americans' perceptions about the role of churches show, church-sponsored events and activities have the potential to help people feel safe and comfortable enough to share openly and honestly about difficult topics such as race, bias, and reconciliation.

* * *

At a recent Q Conference, we were privileged to interview Captain Ronald Johnson, a highway patrol officer from Missouri. If that name doesn't ring a bell, Captain Johnson is the man who was called in to coordinate law enforcement's response to the civil unrest that followed Michael Brown's death. For several days the nation couldn't tear its eyes away from this one man, wondering if he could bring calm to Ferguson or if more violence would erupt between police and protestors.

Captain Johnson became a bridge between two communities who saw the other as an enemy. And like a bridge, he got walked on from both sides. Some among the protesters called him a coward for wearing the uniform. How dare a black man represent the police who were responsible for Michael Brown's death? He was criticized by some in law enforcement for being soft, for marching with protesters, and for apologizing for the police force's initial heavy-handedness.

Others called him courageous.

At Q, Captain Johnson told us that, on one of his first evenings on the job, his young daughter asked, "Daddy, are you scared?"

"Yes, I'm scared," he replied.

The next day his daughter texted a few verses from Matthew 14, where Peter walks on water toward Jesus, along with a message: "When you feel like giving up and you think you are ready to fall remember Jesus is going to pick you up, just like Peter." Those words carried Captain Johnson through the grueling days ahead.

When we asked him what made the ultimate difference in Ferguson, he replied, "The strongest voice that brought calm to Ferguson was the clergy and those of faith that came out and ministered to the citizens of St. Louis. . . . When the law enforcement voice or [school] superintendent's voice . . . could not calm the crowd, the faith of God did."[5] His concluding thought was sobering: "We've gotten to this point [where a Ferguson situation is possible] because we've stepped away from our faith."

Not many of us are in a position to be a Captain Ron Johnson. But good faith Christians of every color can be a bridge that brings together *us and them* to become *we*.

13

THE GAY CONVERSATION

Good faith Christians love
their gay friends and trust
God's design for sexuality.

The moment had finally arrived, the one Gabe had been dreading.

For months, cold sweats and anxious thoughts had accompanied me through the dark hours of the night.

How should I phrase my words?

What do I *really* believe about this?

What questions should I be prepared for?

Could I be making a big mistake?

What on earth was I thinking when I said yes?

But now it was time to step up.

Six months before, I had received a surprising call. A campus minister at Stanford University in Palo Alto, California, was on the line to invite me to be a "conversation partner" on a few topics of interest to the student body. When I read the description of the event, and who I would be having the conversation with, I knew this wouldn't be just a friendly fireside chat.

The description on the Stanford website went something like this:

> In the last year we have seen significant changes in the controversy around LGBT rights. The Supreme Court has struck down the Defense of Marriage Act (DOMA) and California Proposition 8, the military has eliminated Don't Ask, Don't Tell (DADT) and many states have voted to allow same-sex marriage. At the same time, some Christian churches and denominations are also becoming more welcoming and accepting, not only of LGBT ministers, but also of marriage equality. And yet many Christians believe such acceptance of LGBT rights is contrary to scripture and the norms of our tradition. Will this issue tear our churches apart? Is there any room for agreement or reconciliation? Join us for a conversation about the state of family values and marriage equality in the church today.

Against every self-preservation instinct, I accepted.

My conversation partner would be none other than Gene Robinson, the first openly gay Episcopal bishop. The date of our conversation would fall on the tenth anniversary of his consecration to that leadership role. The timing didn't feel like an accident, and it was hard, in those "martyr moments" we all have once in a while, not to feel like a sacrificial lamb.

I spent three months digging in. If I was going to speak publicly on sexuality, gay marriage, and biblical sexual ethics, I wanted to fully know what I believed. Frankly, when I began, I wasn't sure where I would land—I dove in with an open heart and an open mind. I met with scholars, theologians, pastors, and gay friends on all sides of the issues. I read old books and new books, both Christian and secular. I consulted biblical historians, studied first-century culture, and walked my way through two thousand years of church history—all in an effort to understand what our older brothers and sisters in the faith believed in the past, to clarify what I believe in the present, and to communicate those beliefs heading into a contentious future.

And now the evening had arrived. It was time for a conversation most people assumed was already over. It was my opportunity to put my convictions on the line.

Painful Past, Uncertain Future

As we reported in *unChristian*, the attitudes of Christians toward gay people have been damaging to the church's mission. Nine out of ten young people age sixteen to twenty-nine believed, nearly a decade ago, that Christians are antihomosexual. In some sense, their perceptions then were a prediction of the crisis today.

As we begin, we want to reaffirm the culpability of Christians in this, just as we did in our previous book. *Good Faith* is meant to articulate an orthodox view of humans and human sexuality, and part of that orthodoxy is condemning self-righteousness and a spirit of judgmentalism. Can we admit that Christians' treatment of those who identify as gay has contributed to our negative reputation? We've heard stories from teens and adults in the LGBT community who have suffered emotional abuse, physical pain, and social discrimination—at the hands of Christians. Some have even taken their lives. This kind of treatment may not be the norm, but in every case *it is unacceptable. Period.*

If we are honest, we must admit that some Christians (and churches) have had a cruel, homophobic streak. Same-sex attractions and gay sex have been lumped together and treated as the unpardonable sin. As a sexual temptation that affects few parishioners (only 3 or 4 percent of people identify as LGBT[1]), homosexuality has been an easy target. It's an indefensible outlier—not like divorce and remarriage, which are conveniently ignored. With biblical morality as a cover, some Christians have battered the vulnerable LGBT minority with unrelenting condemnation.

Even if we did not actively participate in homophobia—prejudice, hateful words, or even violence because of someone's sexual orientation—many of us were slow to respond to it. We didn't want to "condone" sin by defending sinners, or surrender to the sweeping cultural tide of sexual "freedom," so we stayed silent when we should have challenged our sisters and brothers to put down their stones unless they could honestly say they were without sin.

The next generation noticed the church's sidestepping. They watched (often from the pews) our hypocrisy and too-slow response to LGBT people in our communities.

We must take responsibility for any pain inflicted by Christians on those who experience gay attractions. Children should not be driven to run away from home or contemplate suicide because they were rejected by their family and faith community for feelings outside their control. We must acknowledge and repent of this shameful history.

As we repent of past mistakes, however, we should be cautious. In our rush to make right our wrongs and to restore trust after our failures, we should guard against swinging the pendulum too far in the other direction. In making a commitment to avoid hatefulness, let's not forget any of the ingredients of love + believe + live. We want to love LGBT people, believe the truth about God and the world he created, and live as good faith Christians in relation to this topic—and in relationship with the people it most affects.

Based on our research and what we've been learning, we believe it is possible to be *for* LGBT people *and* to maintain the Christian faith's historic biblical sexual ethic. We don't have to throw faith commitments out with homophobia.

Just as we discovered in the research behind *unChristian*, issues surrounding sexuality are some of the (if not *the*) most significant challenges and opportunities facing the Christian community today. That's why we've devoted three chapters in *Good Faith* to this issue.

Virtually every Christian parent, friend, and pastor wrestles with questions surrounding these topics. With tears and aching hearts in coffee shops, living rooms, dorm rooms, and private prayer closets, anyone who longs to follow Christ and also loves a lesbian, gay, bisexual, or transgender friend or family member has felt the pain of unanswered questions. They struggle to know what to say, what to believe, how to think, and how to stay friends across the gap between deeply held and opposing views. People want to know how they can remain committed to orthodoxy and be a true and loyal friend to LGBT people—and if they are Christians who have same-sex attractions, how to live in a manner that is consistent with what Scripture teaches.

With the utmost care, honesty, and compassion, we hope to clarify the questions so we can move together toward true and life-giving answers. Gabe's story at the beginning of the chapter is one illustration of how we have wrestled with this. We both feel the weight of helping our own families, churches, and organizations think well about the relationship between the church and the LGBT community. We still have a lot to learn. But we hope our transparency and open hearts will help you love, believe, and live a little better too.

Good Sex and the Bible

One of the central questions of our time—as in every age—is how people understand the Bible's authority in relation to their lives and society. Much of what's happening today concerning questions about sex, sexuality, and identity stems from how we think about and orient ourselves toward Scripture.

Frankly, how a person views the authority and accuracy of the Bible is the strongest predictor of what that person believes about homosexuality.

As gay sexuality has become more socially acceptable, Christians have worked hard either to explain a literal interpretation (that a sexual relationship should be only between a married man and woman) or to rationalize the Bible's prohibitions against homosexuality (that gay relationships are a legitimate expression of God's intention for sex).

It is urgent that Christians be able to articulate a strong, rich, vibrant theology of the human body, which includes sex and sexuality, derived from Scripture.

For those who disagree with the historic Christian understanding of these matters, we hope this book will help you to better understand what practicing Christians, and evangelicals in particular, are thinking about, based on our research. Cultural change seems to be happening in fast-forward around us, and we want to slow things down and think together about LGBT issues—and the people behind them! Doing so makes it crystal clear that we desperately need a new way forward on this difficult topic—a way forward that does not comprise orthodox beliefs *or* loving relationships.[2]

Pivoting on the Bible

It is becoming more common to find committed Christians, backed by liberally minded theologians, advocating that the church's affirmation of gay sexual relationships is both inevitable and the right thing to do. These folks have what is described as an "affirming" theology.

While we disagree with their perspective, one of the most emotionally persuasive arguments in favor of affirming LGBT relationships goes something like this:[3]

> Christians used the Bible to defend slavery and oppress black people. They realized later they had interpreted Scripture poorly and so changed their position to be on the right side of history.
>
> Christians are using the Bible to defend traditional marriage and oppress gay people. They are interpreting Scripture poorly again. They will soon change their position to be on the right side of history.

This sounds pretty convincing. After all, if the church messed up on huge issues in the past, who's to say we're not repeating those mistakes? Didn't the church convict Galileo of heresy for arguing, based on science, that the earth is not the center of our universe? What if we are wrong *again*? We meet a lot of leaders who are justifiably worried about the church's poor track record on a range of issues, from science to rights for women and minorities and so on.

However, this argument has a problem: it doesn't account for *history* or align with *Scripture*.

From a historical viewpoint, some Christians have certainly gotten things wrong, but others have gotten things right, often far in advance of the wider culture. In fact, Christians have regularly been a catalyst for positive social change based on their reading of the Bible. Slavery is just one example. Many Christian churches in America's pre–Civil War North set out membership charters, based in part on the theology of the apostle Paul, that connected faith with the abolition of slavery. "All who practice slavery or justify it shall be excluded from the church and its communion."[4] William Wilberforce, the late-eighteenth-century British statesman, rooted his abolitionist movement in the Christian conviction that every human being is made equal in the image of God. Christians—especially younger believers whose passion is based squarely on biblical convictions—make up the critical mass driving today's efforts to end human trafficking (modern-day slavery).

It simply isn't true that Christians are always on the wrong side of history.[5]

Besides, the biggest issue is not guessing at a likely future so we can be on a "right side." That's called peer pressure. Instead, we should be most concerned with Jesus and his purposes today, as best we can discern them.

When it comes to Scripture, the error of the "wrong side of history" argument is that the Bible is counterculturally *for* equal social status for all people created in God's image. Much of Paul's teaching in the New Testament was revolutionary for its time, advocating equality before such an idea was culturally conceivable. "There is no longer Jew or Gentile, slave or free, male and female. For you are all one in Christ Jesus" (Gal. 3:28). His letter to Philemon, a slave owner, does not condone slavery, as one might expect from a writer in first-century culture, but instead presents a countercultural vision for human relationships.[6]

From Genesis to Revelation, the trajectory is toward *more freedom* when it comes to oppressed social groups such as slaves and women.

On human sexuality, the trajectory of Scripture is toward more clarity on God-given constraints—that is, it illuminates a higher, more interconnected set of standards for our sexual lives.

As the story of God's people unfolds—from the Old Testament to Jesus's ministry to the Epistles written to the early church—the Bible's sexual ethic grows clearer and remains in line with the Creator's intentions. Remember when Jesus started with the seventh commandment ("You must not commit adultery") and raised the bar to a higher standard? According to him, entertaining the fantasies of our minds is spiritually on par with committing the sin (see Matt. 5:27–30).

This was and is a revolutionary and countercultural way to think about sex, not because it offers us greater self-fulfillment but because it does just the opposite. Jesus invites us to relinquish self altogether.

More than Right Side, Wrong Side

Those with an affirming theology often try to position them-selves as the counterbalance to the more conservative view and believe their view carries the same historical and theo-logical weight as the historically orthodox perspective. And since more and more people are changing their minds, isn't it just a matter of time before *everyone* does?

Not so fast.

Despite the fast-moving shifts in favor of same-sex mar-riage, our research shows that most practicing Christians are not persuaded.

Americans' Views of Marriage

Which of the following best represents your view of marriage?

	% All Adults	% Practicing Christians	% LGBT
A covenant before God be-tween a man and a woman	51	86	15
A covenant before God be-tween two adults of any gender	13	8	32
A civil agreement between a man and a woman	13	3	4
A civil agreement between two adults of any gender	18	2	44
None of these	5	2	6

Source: Barna OmniPoll, August 2015, N = 1,000

Totals may not equal 100% due to rounding.
Respondents could choose only one option.

- A slim majority of Americans and vast majorities of practicing Christians believe that marriage is a covenant before God between one man and one woman. Further, tens of millions of US adults do not support same-sex marriage; Americans' support for gay marriage dropped from 48 to 42 percent in the month that followed the Supreme Court's *Obergefell* decision.[7]

- Just 28 percent of US practicing Christians and 2 percent of evangelicals support the Supreme Court's decision to legalize same-sex marriage. And while there has been a lot of talk about younger Christians growing more supportive of LGBT rights, the reality is that three-fourths of younger practicing Christians and an even higher proportion of young evangelicals continue to have concerns about the morality of same-sex relationships.

- More than nine out of ten evangelical pastors and 84 percent of Catholic priests contend that the church should "hold to its historic teaching on marriage between one man and one woman." Among mainline pastors,[8] only 55 percent want the church to hold the orthodox line.

- A majority of Mormon, orthodox Jewish, and Muslim leaders also agree that their faith tradition should continue to teach the historic view of marriage as exclusively between one man and one woman. As is the case among Christians, leaders who take their sacred texts to be authoritative seem to be most committed to this view.

- Nine out of ten African American pastors in the United States reject the idea that activism for same-sex marriage rights is similar to the Civil Rights movement of the 1960s.

If you are nonaffirming of gay sexual relationships, you are not alone. But compared to the wider culture, we who hold to biblical sexual ethics *are* considered extreme. We should realize that we face a future in which people have deeply held and passionate opinions that aren't likely to change. This conclusion is not meant to be a threat; it's a simple statement of fact. Some Christians have changed their minds on this issue, and more may do so. But those who work through the arguments on both sides and then remain committed to historic orthodoxy are much less likely to be persuaded.

The political arm of the gay community is likely to keep pushing, even as Christians resist. Astonishingly, one out of five Americans say that clergy should be legally compelled to marry same-sex couples. This isn't a majority view—yet—but it represents the future of this debate.

So we need a way forward through difficult conversations.

While we believe Scripture's sexual standards are quite high, we also believe the Bible compels us to see all people as God's children, made in his image—and that includes gay, lesbian, bisexual, and transgender people.

That's exactly what Gabe had to do when he signed up to be a conversation partner at Stanford University. He worked hard to prepare not for an abstract discussion but for a conversation with a person (Gene Robinson) and the people (the LGBT community) behind the abstractions.

* * *

About sixty minutes before my appointment with Bishop Robinson, I asked my friend Chris to quiz me. I needed a boost of confidence before I publically engaged this tough conversation in front of an audience of young, progressive-minded students.

"Ask me any question on sexual ethics. Anything."

Chris came back, "Why shouldn't two loving people be able to commit to one another for life? Isn't that the most kind and compassionate thing we can do?"

My face felt hot and my hands clammy. "Ah, well, um, I think the way we have to think about this is . . . um, ah . . ." I snapped my mouth shut and thought, *This is going to be a disaster!*

But an hour later, walking onstage, I felt a confident peace that's hard to describe. As a Christian, I knew the source: the Holy Spirit. I had asked God for months to give me the words, to help me be mentally sharp and relationally sensitive, to help me rely on the Spirit's wisdom to engage this difficult topic. Now I felt his presence as I did my best to speak his truth with his love.

It would be absurd to credit every word I said to the divine, so I won't do that. But thanks to that steadying experience of God's presence, I was able to make a few important points that had sometimes been left out of the conversation. Bishop Robinson was smart, fun, and engaging, and graciously gave me space to offer a biblical vision for love, sex, intimacy, identity, and what sin is really all about, and instead of heckling, members of the audience responded with respect and even gratitude. There was a sense in the room that this was a legitimate conversation—not a foregone conclusion—and that the point of view I represented had something significant to contribute to the dialogue.

At the conclusion of the evening, the audience gave a round of applause. As I walked offstage and into a greeting room, dozens of people told Gene and me how much they appreciated the kind, respectful conversation they had just witnessed.

Disagreeing well around this topic is not easy. But on this one night, in this place, it happened. People were genuinely encouraged.

I don't know what results, if any, will come from engaging the public discourse surrounding sexuality and the Christian faith, but I do know God instilled in me that night a conviction that we can trust his design and his ways and that, sometimes, being faithful means showing up for those difficult conversations.

How can we love our LGBT neighbors *and* remain faithful to a biblical sexual ethic? This intersection is a perfect place to live our good faith. Let's talk about how.

14

WE CAN'T LIVE WITHOUT INTIMACY

Good faith Christians welcome
those who are single or celibate
into their households.

Sadly, I have few memories of my brother-in-law, Brian Searles, a handsome, gregarious guy who oozed natural charisma. We just didn't hang out that much.

I remember a couple of times in college when Brian visited his sister, Jill, while on leave from the Air Force.

There was our wedding in 1995, when I gave Brian a Bible as a groomsman's gift. "David, thank you! I've really been wanting to read this more," he said, smiling.

Another time Brian visited us in California for a few days when we were still newlyweds. He brought along his "friend." It didn't dawn on Jill and me until they drove away that they were more than friends. For the first time, we realized Brian was gay.

I remember other brief meetings through the years, mostly at family get-togethers, when Uncle Brian impressed our three kids with his wit and fun-loving nature. During one of those visits, we noticed how much weight he had lost. He didn't look well.

Brian had contracted HIV, which had turned to AIDS. After a painful journey of failed treatments, he passed away in January 2009.

I thought of Brian as a great guy and a good big brother to Jill. But if I am honest, I never really *saw* Brian as anything more than my wife's gay brother.

I'm embarrassed to admit it. It is one of the things I regret most. But it's true.

As we worked on this book and tried to think well about good faith, Gabe and I were convicted by the truth proclaimed by our friend Julie Rodgers, who identifies as a gay Christian: "We can live without sex, but we can't live without intimacy."[1]

I never offered that to my brother-in-law, and it still haunts me. I never tried to understand him or create a deeper friendship with him. What could I have done differently? Might we have been better friends? Why wasn't I more interested in him? Why didn't I spend more time with him when he was sick?

And if Christians are truly committed to the idea of chastity outside of marriage—and I am—why didn't I offer Brian more opportunities for closeness with our family, with his sister, with his nephew and nieces? What if we had invited him to live with us, to become a part of our family's day-to-day life?

In a heartbreaking parody of the good Samaritan, why did my family, the committed Christians, never visit Brian while he was dying, even as his LGBT friends cared for him to his very last breath?

* * *

As straight, married men, we can't speak about same-sex attraction with the authority that comes with firsthand experience. Neither of us has experienced it. Beyond the consequences of sin every person endures, we don't know what it's like to feel fundamentally out of step with family, church, and community, to be the target of gossip or, too often, something darker. The internal anguish that torments our same-sex-attracted Christian friends is awful. And the fact is that many of them, until very recently, faced that anguish alone. It is absolutely essential for Christian communities of faith to walk alongside our sisters and brothers who identify as gay with hearts of compassion and an unwavering commitment to their well-being.

But being gay doesn't come with a different set of rules.

Christianity's biblical sexual ethic is this: sex was designed by God to be between a man and a woman in a covenant marriage. All others are to be celibate or single and sexually chaste, no matter their orientation.

Our research shows that eight out of ten practicing Christians and virtually all evangelicals believe it is "reasonable for Christians to expect fellow Christians who are unmarried to abstain from sex." A majority of US adults across all faith groups agree this is reasonable (56 percent).

In addition, four out of five practicing Christians and nine out of ten evangelicals believe it is "reasonable to expect fellow Christians who experience same-sex attractions to abstain from romantic relationships." Just over half of US adults (52 percent) also believe this is reasonable. Interestingly, younger practicing Christians are just as likely as older Christians to believe these standards of celibacy are reasonable.

About one-third of gay and lesbian adults (across all faith groups, including Christianity), say heterosexual celibacy is reasonable to expect of unmarried Christians. And roughly one out of five of these adults believe it is reasonable for Christians to expect same-sex-attracted Christians to remain celibate. That's lower than the national average, but it still shows that many gay people consider celibacy a viable sexual standard within the Christian community.

Disorientation

Do you have friends or family members who have been aware of their homosexual orientation from their earliest memories? When you hear their stories, it's easy to believe that most gay people didn't choose this path.

Sitting on the stage of the Memorial Church in Palo Alto with Bishop Gene Robinson, I saw the pain in his eyes when he noted that, according to the Catholic Church, "People like me are intrinsically disordered. It's kind of a brick wall. If you are intrinsically disordered, there is not much you can do about that."

Given the opportunity, I responded as gently as I could, "Gene, *I'm* intrinsically disordered. Being a human being with a fallen nature is disordered. I'm *with you*. That is who I am.

That's where I start. We are *all* disordered. We start disordered, and our path to knowing Christ fully is to identify in Christ."[2]

The church has historically taught that same-sex attractions—and plenty of other desires—are disordered as a result of sin. In our politically correct world, however, it's awkward to hear the word *disordered*, much less the word *sin*. And to apply it to a group of people seems hurtful or even hateful. Remember, one of the moral perspectives that is widely embraced is that we should not criticize someone else's life choices, much less call into question their sense of identity. Add to that, most people believe that to find yourself you have to look within yourself.

But the biblical account of human nature is that *we are all disordered*. Relationally disordered, sexually disordered, physically disordered, spiritually disordered . . . just plain disordered. We are all "born that way." The fall of Adam and Eve had consequences; distortion of God's design is one of them. Not every longing is a desire God intended us to experience. You can't find who you are simply by actualizing your desires— gay, straight, bisexual, transgender, or whatever.

The intricate blend of nurture, nature, and environment is a powerful, but mysterious, force on sexuality. Most prominent LGBT advocates and the American Psychological Association acknowledge that the origins of sexual orientation are not a known science.[3, 4] A homosexual orientation may include a genetic, physiological component (as many LGBT activists insist) that is then catalyzed by childhood experiences. It seems to be true that every person's sexuality is fluid up to a certain age; a variety of influences have the potential to nest or take flight. In Jenel Williams Paris's *The End of Sexual Identity*, she writes, "Scholars today agree that there are not two or three separate 'types' of humans, sexually speaking. Instead, there are ranges of behavior, fluidity in sexual feelings and complicated personal sexual histories."[5]

To pretend to understand all the dynamics would be to play God. The delicate mix of nurture and nature is so complex that only the Creator can understand how each individual's sexuality takes shape. We humbly suggest that trying to find a single answer to disordered human desire is a dead-end road. Rather, it's more helpful just to acknowledge that most people who experience a lesbian or gay sexual orientation didn't choose it. It is all they've ever known.

When the disciples asked Jesus whose sin was at fault to make a man blind—the man's parents' sin or his own—Jesus told them they were asking the wrong question (see John 9). According to the Lord, the right question, in essence, was, *How is God revealing his purposes in and through this man's life?*

That's the question we must ask today.

Good News for *Everyone*

For many Christians with same-sex attractions who tried to become "ex-gay," the "good news" was synonymous with experiencing a complete orientation change. For some, that meant becoming heterosexual and being happily married to a person of the opposite sex. Anything else felt "less" or insufficient. But while a small percentage of people *do* report such a shift of their sexual attractions away from the same sex and toward the opposite sex, it is not a common experience.[6] We trust that transformation in Christ brings freedom from the old self. But how do we walk alongside brothers and sisters whose same-sex attractions don't shift, or don't shift quickly? Their presence among us begs the question: is the American dream of a nuclear family really the only place the gospel leads us?

No.

We fundamentally misunderstand the good news of Jesus if "happily married with two kids" is our first picture of salvation. Or, for that matter, if we say the good news for *anyone* is about finding a fulfilling sexual relationship.

When we make the good news about going straight or getting married or having fulfilling sex lives, but then most gay people don't experience full transformation of their desires as part of their "salvation," they are understandably sent reeling. It is no wonder that many look for other ways to sort out their confused reality and satisfy their good human desire for lifelong companionship.

Can we blame them? Walking a day in their shoes, we would be tempted to do the same. Feeling trapped and isolated, this is the story for many Christians who have decided that living out their gay sexual desires is not in conflict with Scripture.

We have listened to many friends describe their angst and agony. The common narrative goes something like this: "If I have gay feelings, God must want me to . . . after all, he made me. And if he made me and I have these feelings, he wouldn't want me to repress these feelings and experience internal conflict about following him. So he must think it's okay to be gay. We must have gotten something wrong in how we've interpreted Scripture."

This is an oversimplified version of a typical story and is in no way meant to devalue the earnest searching that drives some LGBT Christians to try to harmonize their sexual desires with their longing to follow Christ. But reading Scripture solely through the lens of our personal experiences is a dead end.

It's not only LGBT Christians looking for new interpretations, but their friends too: about nine out of ten Americans say they personally know someone who is gay,[7] and those relational bonds can be a powerful motivator for people to reexamine their beliefs about what Scripture does and does not say.

A growing number of Americans believe their feelings should dictate their identity. A good faith Christian's identity, however, is found in Christ.

Our identity is not found by looking within.

God designed human identity to be found and fulfilled in a fixed point outside ourselves—in him. He beckons us toward his plan for our flourishing, toward what's truly best for our hearts, minds, and bodies. *This* is good news, for gay people and everyone else!

When we understand who we are as God's children and image-bearers, created to glorify him by becoming more like his Son, we experience our deepest fulfillment.

In fulfilling God's purposes, we find our purpose.

Philosopher, scholar, and Roman Catholic Charles Taylor made the case three decades ago that America's new religion is self-fulfillment. In his book *The Ethics of Authenticity*, he claims, "We set an overwhelmingly high value on self-fulfillment, on the idea that each of us should find some way of life that satisfies us and is authentically our own."[8] He goes further in diagnosing how we lost our way:

> The rise of individualism has wrenched us loose from all the settings that gave meaning to the lives of our forebears; we have been thrown back on our inner resources, but when we look inside ourselves, we find emptiness because we have been cut adrift from everything that once supplied the resources we are seeking.[9]

Our society has cut itself adrift from the wisdom and knowledge of the ages. In the pursuit of progress, we've forgotten what life is all about.

As we argued in chapter 4, Christians believe life is *not* about self-fulfillment but about glorifying God and fulfilling his purpose to restore our relationships, our communities, and ourselves.

This is good news.

Our Identity in Christ

The world celebrated and debated the introduction of Caitlyn, Bruce Jenner's transformed self. America's athlete—the 1976 Olympic gold medal winner of the decathlon and official spokesman for Wheaties cereal—felt deep inside that he was a she. Years of mental anguish and soul searching led Jenner to decide he could no longer live as a man.

We are not at all callous toward the transgender experience. We feel sadness and compassion for those on this journey. Watching Jenner's "coming out" interview with Diane Sawyer, we were moved by the former Olympian's story. We also think there are huge lessons the church can learn (or remember) when engaging family, friends, and fellow believers who experience this disordered reality. Honestly, the urging of the trans community to look beyond superficiality and physicality to see a human soul inspires us. Many of the transgender people we've encountered ask bigger, more significant, questions than those who feel at home in their own skin about what it means to be human. This is good.

Christians must not be hard-hearted toward those who seek alternate identities. Their quest is a signpost pointing to a deep desire to be truly, profoundly known.

But we can offer timeless truth when it comes to how highly our culture values *feelings*. As Charles Taylor wrote, culture persuades us to find out who we are by looking within, at how we feel deep down.[10] But feelings are not always to be trusted. They offer us important information about our internal disposition toward reality, but they themselves aren't reality—and, on occasion, they directly contradict it. This is why Christians root our identity in something real. Humans need a fixed point outside ourselves that helps us know who we are, against which we can measure how well our feelings reflect reality.[11]

Our identity, calling, and purpose come from a source outside ourselves. When we do not submit our feelings to that source, to the Spirit of God, we risk deceiving ourselves.

In a video promoting Caitlyn's introduction to the world in *Vanity Fair*, Jenner says, "As soon as [the cover] comes out, I'm free."[12] How sad. This is the enemy's lie. The ultimate deception is that freedom can be found in chains. All the makeup, pretty dresses, and photo shoots in the world can't free a person from bondage to feelings.

In a world where gender confusion abounds, distorted sexual desires and behaviors are celebrated, and the title "hero" is bestowed on those who live according to their feelings, the deceiver is having a field day.

Fulfillment is just around the corner.

My life will be better when I'm in charge of my own destiny.

I'll be happy if I can make reality match my feelings.

The lies are as old as Eden's tree.

How can Christians of good faith compete with the majority culture's message, "To find yourself look within"? After all, valuing unique personalities, experiences, dreams, gifts, and points of view is a good thing. But it's not the *first* thing. As C. S. Lewis wrote, "You can't get second things by putting them first; you can get second things only by putting first things first."[13]

Christians must properly order first and second things.

But society's uproar only gets louder, pointing people in the opposite direction. Tim Keller says our culture "presses its members to believe 'you have to be yourself,' that sexual desires are crucial to personal identity, that any curbing of strong sexual desires leads to psychological damage."[14] Or as Taylor Swift sings, you can "want who you want."

This commonly held belief has become a kind of religion: *to be fulfilled you must actualize your desires.* But if we want to be people of good faith, we must distinguish good ideas from bad ideas and live our lives accordingly.

Self-fulfillment is a bad idea, a dead end.

We don't have to blindly go along with the majority culture's reliance on feelings to discover the truth about ourselves. Instead, we can shed light on the distortions and offer a vision of wholeness and true identity found in Christ.

People to Be Loved

Our friend Preston Sprinkle has a great phrase for how Christians should respond to LGBT people, Christian or otherwise: *as people to be loved.*[15]

People.

To.

Be.

Loved.

Not an issue to be solved.

As we have said throughout this book, good faith is living out our love for others and our belief in God's good ways.

It's easy to think that sex and sexuality can be boiled down to knowing what we believe, and to forget loving altogether.

That's what Simon the Pharisee does, as recorded in Luke 7. He is at a dinner where Jesus is the guest of honor, and an immoral woman crashes the party. She makes an inappropriate scene by kissing Jesus's feet and begging his forgiveness.

Simon knows what he believes about the woman's sins but doesn't see a person to be loved. His thoughts betray him: "If this man were a prophet, he would know what kind of woman is touching him. She's a sinner!" (v. 39).

Contrary to Simon's assumptions, Jesus knows and does not overlook the woman's broken history. He even tells the dinner guests that her sins are "many." But he doesn't do so to rub her face in her past. He says it to show that his forgiveness can restore even the most broken of people.

Jesus restores people today, including refugees of the sexual revolution. He restores people through the church, the properly functioning household of God that loves, believes, and lives good faith.

Some people wonder when we should offer our love to people far from God, and when we should withhold it. This is an important question. Remember that Jesus loved us, enough to die, *while we were still sinners.* So while there will always be consequences of sin, including church discipline for those within the Christian community, those consequences should never exclude someone from love.

If you're a Christian, offering people love is as basic as breathing.

Has a friend confessed his addiction to porn? Even if this disappoints you, he is a person to be loved.

Did your daughter come out as a lesbian? She is a person to be loved.

Has someone in your church gotten pregnant outside of marriage? She is a mom-to-be to be loved.

Is a young couple in your church living together outside of marriage? They are people to be loved.

As we begin to see people for who they are—created in the image of God—we think less of LGBT issues to be solved and instead see people to be loved. When we don't, bad faith can creep in and distort Christ's ongoing work of restoration within the Christian community.

Jesus went out of his way to reorient people to a new religious order. He called out religious leaders who avoided the marginalized members of society and taught their communities to do the same. The ostracized were destined to live lonely, scared, and painful lives, banished from safety, community, and intimacy.

Jesus flipped this upside down, and the marginalized were his choice to receive miracles and blessing. As Jesus healed and then welcomed them back into the community, their lives bore witness to the new order that indicted the old, revealing the ungodly legalism and self-righteousness that had taken deep root in God's people.

Today's questions surrounding sex and sexuality can be a gift. When the biblical sexual ethic calls our sisters and brothers attracted to the same sex to deny themselves, they model how the wider church already ought to be living.

Instead of singling out this one area of self-denial, what if we raise the stakes for everyone to live costly obedience?

The lives of single and celibate Christians give testimony to the kind of self-denial many of us have forgotten. Reflecting on their lives—on the people we love—we ought to be convicted and pressed to consider, *What appetites am I denying myself for Jesus's sake? Is discipleship costing me anything?*

For many of us, the answer is no.

Most modern North American Christians have little imagination for self-denial. Who can blame us? The thousands of marketing messages we receive every day reinforce the idea that we should deny ourselves nothing, that we deserve to consume more, that seeking our own pleasure leads to "the good life."

But self-denial is essential to following Jesus. The familiar command to

> "Take up your cross and follow me"
> begins with
> "turn from your selfish ways"
> and ends with a warning
> "if you try to hang on to your life, you will lose it"
> and a promise
> "if you give up your life for my sake, you will save it."[16]

It doesn't make sense to a self-centered society that thinks denying our desires is extreme, but self-denial is part and parcel of good faith. As Paul wrote to the church in Corinth, "'I have the right to do anything,' you say—but not everything is beneficial" (1 Cor. 6:12 NIV). Acknowledging and living within God's boundaries is not crazy. Weird, sure. But not crazy.

Christians in our churches who are committed to the biblical sexual ethic are living, breathing examples of the self-denial required by Jesus of those who want to be his disciples. The faithful lives of single and celibate Christians, gay or straight, are a call to the entire church to live out *costly* obedience—even when it hurts.

Church as "First Family"

The apostle Peter calls all exiles "to abstain from sinful desires, which wage war against your soul" (1 Pet. 2:11 NIV), but self-denial was never meant to be practiced in isolation. Through the presence of the Holy Spirit and our brothers and sisters in Christ, we are meant to live out costly obedience in close communion with God and others.

This is true for us all but especially for single Christians. As theologian Dayna Olson-Getty cautions, "To say 'no' to something as powerfully magnetic as sex requires something even more powerful to which one is saying 'yes.'"[17] Expanding our vision to see the church as our first family is critical . . . and biblical. We can't ask gay Christians to deny themselves the intimacy of a close sexual relationship without offering the intimacy of close godly relationships.

In Eve Tushnet's memoir, *Gay and Catholic*, she writes, "Knitting single people more closely into families is one of the biggest things the Christian churches could do."[18] She speaks directly to the need of the day: for the church to become a family for those who don't feel a part of one. As just one example of how this could look, Tushnet points to the blog of Matthew Jones, who relates the joyful experience of attending a straight friend's wedding:

> After I came out to the groom, he sent me a letter explaining how, even should I never have a family of my own, I had to know that I would always be a part of theirs—that I was someone they wanted their kids to know and learn from. They have demonstrated that their love for each other somehow includes *me*. . . . [At their wedding] I caught the slightest glimpse of a future spent never too far from a warm living room full of people who will gladly call me brother and friend.[19]

Tushnet offers practical suggestions for making church a safe and welcoming place for same-sex-attracted Christians to belong.[20] One of the most important is to "talk about gay issues with a spirit of welcome." She writes:

> If your church has a moment when you can add a public prayer, you might pray for God to bless gay, lesbian, and/or same-sex attracted people. Or you could pray that all people, regardless of sexual orientation, will find their vocation as they learn to give and receive love. Similarly, a lot of spiritual topics have some aspect that is especially relevant to gay or same-sex at-tracted people. If you're talking about "guardianship of the tongue," why not include homophobic slurs as something to avoid along with gossip and jokes at other people's expense? If you're talking about how God the Father can offer a model of fatherhood for those whose earthly fathers aren't too loving, why not include the fathers who reject their gay children? There are countless little ways to indicate that you know that gay and same-sex attracted people are part of the Body of Christ.[21]

All LGBT Christians need to know their church recognizes and celebrates the gifts they bring to the community. We must welcome them into our homes and family life and support the unique contributions they make to fulfilling God's purposes. Because they might never enter into a covenant marriage with a person of the opposite sex, their church family must be ex-actly that: *family*.

For many young Americans, a church community does not present an obvious solution to their lack of stable family con-nections. Only 44 percent of unchurched adults are married, compared to nearly six out of ten churchgoers. Three out of ten churchless Americans have never been married, compared to 20 percent of churchgoing adults.

Our society feels the very real need for family, yet it seems that families are more comfortable than singles in church.

You can be a gift to same-sex-attracted and other single people in your church by changing your everyday, ordinary rhythms to involve them. For families with children, it could mean inviting a single friend over for a weekly movie or pizza night. Include them in holiday get-togethers and bestow on them "aunt" and "uncle" honors for your children. Invite those without an immediate nuclear family to experience the joys, hardships, and routine patterns of family life.

They, in turn, will be a gift to you. You can take friendship out of the virtual and put it back in the real world, sharing the ups and downs of daily life with a sister or brother who sees past your filtered profile picture (and loves you anyway). Your children will have a trusted, godly adult other than you and your spouse to mentor, care for, and be a friend to them.

This will not always be easy. (Relationships never are.) But it is a vision for church as first family, as we explored in chapter 10.

A more nuanced (and biblical) theology of the family and a more robust theology of singleness and celibacy will allow the church to gain a more credible position on the joys and hardships of living the biblical sexual ethic. Only as the family of God can we credibly call gay and bisexual Christians to celibacy. If we do not reconfigure our churches to be communities that welcome, support, and celebrate singleness, we are asking gay and straight brothers and sisters to do hard, lifelong work without the willingness to do so ourselves.

"God places the lonely in families," Psalm 68:6 says. Are we teaching straight Christian couples a wide-enough view of family, wide enough to enfold sisters and brothers who are single and those answering God's call to celibacy? Asking single Christians to remain chaste on their own is not biblical. We must not ask them to carry this burden alone.

We *all* need intimacy. And when we live into Jesus's vision of the church as family, we can find it in each other.

15

FIVE WAYS TO BE FAITHFUL

Good faith Christians
thoughtfully engage the most
divisive issues of our time.

Before the Supreme Court decision that made same-sex marriage legal nationwide, I recall watching a well-known pastor on national television struggle to answer a reporter's question. "Do you support New York's gay marriage legislation?"

"As the Bible teaches us," he replied, "I believe marriage is between a man and a woman, and any other arrangement is out of step with God's best. Of course I don't support so-called gay marriage!"

Convinced she had just interviewed another Bible-thumper with no concept of what it means to live in a pluralistic culture, the reporter shrugged and introduced the next segment.

At first glance, the pastor's response may seem perfectly fine—faithful even. And that's why it is a good example of the confusion surrounding how Christians should engage this complex topic. Whether on TV or at a backyard barbecue, when we're asked a *political* question, our knee-jerk reaction is often to give a *theological* response. Clear theology matters, of course, and it should color how we see everything about the world. But how we apply that theology to specific situations requires not only theological knowledge but also prayerful wisdom.

The pastor on TV is not alone. In Barna's survey of US clergy, only about half of Protestant and Catholic ministers report feeling very well prepared to address political questions surrounding same-sex marriage and other LGBT rights. We believe figuring this out is an urgent matter of good faith. Our inability to parse the various facets of the debate muddles our message.

If you're not aware of the religious freedom debates that have erupted over the past couple of years around pizza shop owners (Indiana), pastry chefs (Colorado and Oregon), wedding venue operators (New York), and photographers (Arizona) who have objected, on religious grounds, to furnishing their services for gay weddings, you probably don't have an internet connection. Many LGBT activists are yelling, "Discrimination!" and comparing such objections of conscience to "Jim Crow laws."[1] Meanwhile, some Christians are wondering if, instead of objecting, serving a gay couple's wedding ceremony could actually be the best way to demonstrate love, kindness, and a desire for friendship.

Who's right? Who's wrong?

What if we could break this down and understand each of the dynamics at play? What if we could separate the politics from Christian theology and understand how our hearts for ministry can engage with new realities in the public square? We recognize that good theology impacts every other decision we make, but is there room for freedom on how to *live* and *love* well even if most practicing Christians agree on what to *believe*? Good faith can sort out the confusion, and instead of always giving the same "Christian answer," good faith Christians can faithfully address the questions people are really asking.

The following framework, which we might describe as five lenses through which we can view our response to LGBT people and related topics, gives Christians a way to see through the fog. These lenses not only help us think clearly about the current sexuality debate but also provide a framework for how good faith believers can respond to current issues and to future issues that arise.

Theology	What does God's Word and the church's wisdom reveal about this?
Ministry	What is the proper pastoral response to people living in a fallen world?
Relationships	How should I engage friends and neighbors with whom I disagree?
Politics	What government policies, however imperfect, best empower human flourishing?
Public Square	What is the appropriate relationship between personal conviction and day-to-day interactions with those who hold different sets of beliefs?

While this framework won't ease the burden of believing something vastly different than the dominant culture, we believe it clarifies the issues and gives good faith Christians a way forward.

Good faith Christians place the highest value on God's view of any matter. Our theology should be top priority, rooted first in God's Word, then bolstered by the church's historic teaching, and, finally, buoyed by reason and experience. Pastors across the nation seem to broadly share this priority, with more than eight out of ten Protestant and Catholic ministers saying they feel well prepared to address theological questions related to LGBT issues.

Once we know what we believe, we should allow freedom for *how* Christ-followers apply theology to their own engagement with people, politics, and the public square. Christians will not always agree on the details of how best to *live* orthodox *belief*, so we need grace to allow for differences of opinion and differences in how the Spirit leads each of us to love our neighbor. Being dogmatic or prescriptive about *second* things—ministry, relationships, politics, and the public square—drives an unnecessary wedge between Christians and gives reasons for the watching world to question our unity. Let's major on the majors (orthodox theology) and bless each other's efforts to be faithful on the minors.

Theology

I was having coffee several years ago with the late Chuck Colson, a key mentor in my life and a stalwart in calling Christians to engage well with the wider culture. I asked him, "How should the church be thinking about all of these new issues that are raising so much debate? Like immigration, war, homosexuality, the environment, and so on?"

With a piercing look, Chuck said, "Gabe, you know these aren't new issues, right?" With a wry smile and a fatherly tone, he continued, "Our church fathers dealt with every one of these issues. There isn't anything new your generation will deal with that hasn't already been wrestled down by the church. These aren't new issues; they are old ideas that recycle through history. Sure, they may present themselves today as more or less acceptable or extreme, but they aren't new." And before I could get a word in, he jibed, "You really should read more old books, Gabe!"

That conversation was the kick in the pants I needed to go deeper, to stop assuming every issue in the twenty-first century is a special case requiring yet another reexamination of Scripture. We Protestants have a short history—evangelicals, even shorter. In my search for old books, I came across the Catholic Church's *Compendium of the Social Doctrine of the Church*, a large volume that synthesizes Catholic teaching on most every issue in culture, a compilation of wisdom from throughout the ages. Overwhelmed by the profound, timeless insights, I was reminded how rich a heritage we share with our Catholic brothers and sisters. And especially as we look to the days ahead, let's not forget it. Tried and true wisdom can benefit us all.

Christians (and Muslims and Jews) have believed for millennia that sex is for one man and one woman inside a covenant marriage. In all other cases, we are to remain celibate or single and chaste.

Christopher Yuan, a transformed believer whose past includes gay prostitution, says that celibacy is a choice, but singleness is each person's origin and destiny. "Few people are called to celibacy but everyone *was* single (at birth), *is* single (through their childhood and young adult years), and in the end *will be* single (in heaven). . . . Celibacy is a commitment; singleness is a state of being."[2] Some Christ-followers are called to celibacy as a vocation, but all single believers are called to chastity.

This vision for sexuality applies to every person, desire, and category. Gay, bisexual, straight, married, single, or other—everyone bears the same burden. For some, this may seem a heavier weight to carry, but, nonetheless, God's design for sexuality applies equally to each person.

All Christians—not just lesbian, gay, bisexual, and transgender believers—are called by God to extraordinarily high standards of moral behavior. God's calling on same-sex-attracted Christians is just one part of a holistic sexual ethic that applies to each of us who takes up a cross to follow Christ.

With this in mind, let's acknowledge that Christians who hold to biblical sexual ethics are—compared to the wider culture at least—extreme. And so, to some extent, we should get comfortable with the label "extremist." Increasingly, it will be applied to biblically committed Christians not for assassinating abortionists or carrying "God Hates Fags" signs at funerals (legitimately extreme) but for holding deep religious convictions that don't align with the majority culture's dogma.

Jesus never said the word *homosexuality*. What he *did* say about marriage and divorce, however, illuminates a consistent sexual ethic. So, for example, when the Pharisees ask Jesus if it is "lawful for a man to divorce his wife for any and every reason" (Matt. 19:3 NIV), he uses the occasion to teach.

> At the beginning the Creator "made them male and female," and said, "For this reason a man will leave his father and mother and be united to his wife, and the two will become one flesh." . . . They are no longer two, but one flesh. Therefore what God has joined together, let no one separate. (Matt. 19:4–6 NIV)

Teaching against the current of religious loopholes and legal double-dealing, Jesus taught a sexual ethic that was narrow and tight, not broad and loose. He took his listeners back to the beginning, back to his created order, back to his design for human flourishing.

Some who have adopted an affirming theological approach believe that Jesus's reference to Genesis doesn't explicitly exclude same-sex monogamous commitments. They argue that his vision for "one flesh" could mean an "indissoluble kinship bond that shouldn't be torn apart by divorce,"[3] and, therefore, same-sex marriage shouldn't be prohibited based on his statement.

But Jesus's reference to the Creator making them "male and female" affirms God's design for sexual difference in marriage. As our friend Preston Sprinkle has written, "If Jesus didn't think that sexual difference is essential for marriage, then his quotation of Genesis 1:27, which talks about sexual difference, is unnecessary and superfluous. But Jesus does quote it, so it would seem that male-female pairing is part of what marriage is according to Jesus."[4] Jesus's words reassert God's design for male and female union. Any other sexual union falls short of his design for human flourishing.

This is what Christians have believed and aspired to practice for more than two thousand years. And Jews for many more.

But a new generation is questioning this wisdom. They are experiencing a crisis of belief, questioning whether they can trust the authority of Scripture and the church's timeless wisdom.

When there is this much confusion, we must go back to the basics.

In the beginning, God created people in his own image, male and female. They were created as two opposite halves of a perfect whole, designed to come together in marriage. In a marriage, these two sexually different people form a union and, together, reflect God's creation order. Marriages create nuclear and extended families, which have always been the building blocks of clan, tribe, neighborhood, city, and nation. Extended families and households, as described earlier, are the fundamental ingredient for human communities. These are the basics.

These principles represent God's intention, and we must aim for that ideal in a fractured and disordered world. While some people may be quick to dispose of it, good faith Christians recognize that, even if this understanding of heterosexual marriage is unpopular, the Bible's teaching and two thousand years' worth of Christian wisdom means something.

Ministry

Our ministry approach must be *pastoral*—that is, it must shepherd each person toward a deeper love for Christ through the distortions and brokenness all human beings experience. With complete freedom, Christians should show Christ's unconditional love to LGBT people in their lives. For some, this might mean hanging out at gay bars like my friend Chris, who is known as the unofficial "chaplain" for his city's lesbian community. He's on every guest list for every party. They love him. He loves them and shows it with his presence.

Beyond the important work of building relationships outside the church, how do we minister to Christians with same-sex attraction in our churches? There is only one way. We must create church cultures that reflect the culture of God's kingdom. A kingdom culture fulfills relational longings far deeper than sexual desire.

As we touched on in previous chapters, Christians should be careful not to make marriage an idol, assuming it is every believer's destiny. Instead, we need to cast a compelling vision for the value and vocations of single people. We must not define significance or maturity in terms of marital status. Instead, we must reorient our community's values around spiritual gifts and service. At the same time, we must challenge married couples to open their lives and homes to those who don't have families of their own. The church is every Christian's first family, and this truth should be felt most intensely by those who are not or never will be married. Remember, we can live without sex but not without intimacy.

In a kingdom culture, people experiencing same-sex attractions feel welcomed, find community where they can belong, and discover a life's calling aimed at God's purposes.

They hear stories of other single and celibate Christians celebrated.

They are reminded, with their fellow congregants, of their first identity in Christ and are equipped to answer his call to become like him.

They experience a recovery of deep, lasting, Christian friendship.

One word of caution: while there should be great freedom in how Christians engage in ministering to the LGBT community, in what direction we choose to minister and pastorally care for people ought to reflect our theology. To take an obvious example: because we believe the church's historic sexual ethic requires our single friends to remain chaste regardless of their attractions, we wouldn't encourage them to pursue a sexual relationship.

In practical terms, churches committed to the biblical sexual ethic may draw clear lines that ensure theological and lifestyle alignment for those in church leadership or a discipleship role. This may at first glance appear harsh or insensitive, but consistency of practice leads to more clarity for those who are confused about how to love, believe, and live as good faith Christians.

Various churches will have different ways of relating and ministering to Christians who identify as gay. Our pastor friend Dean Curry explains why his church does baby dedications for gay couples' children:

> Baby dedications, as we do them today, are not in the Bible. We made them up to say we believe this child is blessed. So if it really is about the child, then we want to keep it focused on the child. Forget gay or straight—we dedicate people's children all the time whose parents may be in sin. We don't ask of heterosexuals, "Are they qualified to be great parents?" or "Are they living spotless lives?" before we bless their child. It's a moot point for us what the parent is up to because it is about the child. . . . When two women come to us and say, "Would you dedicate our child?" we say, "Absolutely. We believe this child is blessed and a work of art by God, and we are going to pray his best over this child."[5]

There are many practical questions with which pastors are wrestling. What if an already-married gay couple starts attending your church? How do you minister to them? And what if they have children? Leaders can and will disagree on how to best answer these kinds of questions, even as they hold to an orthodox theological position. That's partly the point. The ministry lens should be viewed with some latitude because people are trying to work out the implications of theology within their communities.

These questions and the need for latitude should not be used as an excuse to be unclear about your church's beliefs. We do a grave disservice to those who are gay and seeking to follow Jesus if we hide away the uncomfortable parts of the biblical message on sexuality. Being upfront about your community's beliefs regarding God's vision for sexual flourishing—without harping on it constantly—can prevent all kinds of misunderstandings and relational strife. When churches are *not* clear, gay couples are justified in their anger at what feels like a "bait and switch": they've invested themselves in the community yet never once heard the church does not affirm gay sexual relationships. That's a rude surprise, and it can be avoided with kind, clear teaching on matters of sexuality.

At a minimum, we should agree that the basic unit of ministry is the person, meaning that our ministry efforts should never do harm to people—especially young people—who are searching God's truth about their sexuality. If our churches can't be the safest place on the planet for people to talk about their feelings and experiences and to find themselves in Christ, our churches aren't doing ministry the way Jesus did.

Relationships

Many people—perhaps you—aren't dealing with these tensions at the church or ministry level. Instead, they just want to know how to talk with their friends, family members, and neighbors with whom they disagree. As majority culture normalizes gay relationships and minimizes gender differences, we need to know how and how *not* to talk about such things.

Gabe learned the hard way how difficult those conversations can be.

One evening Rebekah and I were having dinner with a couple we had enjoyed getting to know for a few years. The husband, Bill, is a news media personality, and his wife, Maria, is a doctor. Somehow Bill and I found ourselves knee deep in a conversation about where the gay sexuality question is headed in the US church. We were in the habit of discussing social issues, so this wasn't unusual. Bill knew I was familiar with the attitudes of a younger generation of Christians, and I knew he was interested in understanding the topic more deeply. He was asking me questions in a matter-of-fact tone, and I was giving him the pulse of where I thought things are headed. Since he's in the journalism business, the factual tone and content of our conversation seemed perfectly normal to us both.

But at a certain point, Bill's wife, Maria, overheard an off-handed comment I made describing the theory that children aren't born gay but that a mix of nature, nurture, and environment likely plays a role in the development of sexual orientation and gender identity. Maria interrupted, "That's not true!" There were tears in her eyes and layers of tension in her voice.

Taken off guard, I asked for her to tell me more. "My nephew, who is only four years old, thinks he's a girl. He loves twirling around in ballerina dresses and playing with dolls. My brother is a man's man. It sounds like you're saying it's his fault my nephew thinks he's a girl."

"Oh no . . . I'm so sorry. I had no idea."

But the damage was done. My insensitivity had hurt the relationship. Although there was no way I could have known Maria's story, I walked away sad and frustrated that I'd possibly hurt our budding friendship because I'd spoken too casually and made sexuality and gender identity an "issue"—not about real people.

I learned an important lesson: when it comes to relationships, tone matters as much as—if not more than—substance. Christians should be the most loving, kind, respectful, and teachable friends, always going the extra mile to understand, to listen, and to give grace far beyond what is expected.

So many in the LGBT community, and among their families, harbor anger toward the church because of the judgmental spirit levied by some Christians toward family members and friends. When this is the case, it takes extra effort to build relational bridges. If you aren't already a friend to someone who is gay, proactively seek those friendships, regardless of your theological differences. Humbly confess and acknowledge the cruel, homophobic, and dehumanizing attitudes that have been too prevalent among Christians. Listen to and empathize with people's very personal stories. Trying to understand another person's point of view is not the same as endorsing it. It's being a friend.

I sent an email to Bill later that evening apologizing profusely once again for my insensitivity and asking him to relay my apologies to Maria. He was gracious and told me no major damage had been done. It was just tough timing on this particular topic. He and Maria would forgive and forget.

Discussing an issue that needs to be solved is trivial compared to encountering a person who needs to be known.

Orientations bent toward heterosexuality or homosexuality matter little. God sees all of us as his children, whom he desperately longs for and wants to renew. He wants to bring each of us into alignment with his purpose. If we can't see the "other" this way—as a child of God with emotions, needs, scars, and desires—we cannot truly know or be known.

Engaging with a spirit of humility will create opportunities for a new beginning with those we love most.

Politics

Perhaps the toughest arena to engage, on any issue today, is politics. But it's essential to get our bearings with realistic expectations for how to be faithful in this contentious sphere of life.

When it comes to politics, the job of the church is not primarily to win legislative victories but to bear witness to God's kingdom.[6] It's true that some Christians are called into politics, and it's certainly not a bad thing to want laws that help our society flourish. We should advocate for those. But it's easy to overemphasize the importance of politics and downplay the power of relationships.

Our theology should not be divorced from our politics, but we need to be clear about which is which. Theology is our best understanding of God's revelation. Politics is about making wise and prudent decisions in a particular context. Theological reflection can and must inform our politics, but let's also acknowledge that Christians in other contexts may come to different political conclusions after their own process of theological reflection.

Good faith Christians should give one another freedom to hold different views and positions when it comes to political participation.

Ross, a friend of Gabe's, believes Christians should be on the front lines of the fight for legislation that would protect LGBT citizens from housing or employment discrimination.

But another friend, Joelle, is adamant that LGBT citizens already enjoy all the rights of any other citizen, and should not be legally classified as a specially protected class. Doing so, she believes, would wrongly equate the LGBT cause with the Civil Rights movement, which sought to dismantle centuries of government-sanctioned white supremacy.

As you can see, good faith Christians will disagree on how to best engage politically—and that's okay.

It is not the church's job to secure law and legal policy that reflect biblical morality. Our mission is to live as citizens of God's coming kingdom and, in so doing, proclaim what God intended and desires for his creation.[7]

Public Square

As most Christians recognize, our ways of thinking no longer dominate the public square. Gabe argued in his book *The Next Christians* that this change will ultimately be good for the church.[8]

The reality is that the space where we coexist with people who hold different views is becoming more turbulent. In the years ahead, Christians must learn how to share a public square with those who vehemently disagree with us. One important way we can do so is to look for common cause with those who otherwise oppose us. For example, there are plenty of issues related to LGBT rights that can divide Christians from the majority. Yet with good faith, we can find some common ground.

Over the last few years, I have developed a friendship with Andrew Sullivan, widely considered one of the heroes of the gay rights movement. He understands politics and the public square like few people I've ever known. In the 1980s, long before it occurred to anyone else, he implored the LGBT community to accept nothing short of marriage in its pursuit of full acceptance in the wider society.

As we anticipated the *Obergefell* Supreme Court decision, Andrew and I intentionally engaged in conversation about how we could model respect and friendship despite differences around such polarizing issues. He kindly accepted my invitation to join us at our Q Boston national gathering, where together we discussed how to find common ground.

In an unexpected moment of grace, Andrew publicly apologized for the times members of his community had pushed Christian leaders and institutions too far in pursuit of advancing their rights. I did the same, confessing the ways the church has not understood the LGBT community's painful experiences with Christians. We both expressed a desire to ensure that each person, on whatever side, is humanized, even if there is disagreement on God's best.

There are simple, clear ways to live good faith in this arena. For example, we can all agree that no child should be subjected to bullying, the target of constant name-calling, social shaming, or even physical violence. All parents ought to have confidence that the community of leaders is looking out for their child. To push back the tide of bullying that has overrun sexual minorities in schools and local communities, we can make common cause with LGBT activists. We can join with groups that give voice to the problem and call for accountable leaders to protect kids who are most at risk.

Another area where we can find common alignment is condemning discrimination against those in the LGBT community. When it comes to housing and employment, sexual orientation or identity should not prevent access. There can and should be robust debate about whether to legislate special protections for LGBT citizens, but these are basic, fundamental rights all Americans enjoy, and Christians should not hesitate to side with people who have been marginalized and excluded from these rights.

Having said that, as gay rights become more commonplace, it will be equally important to allow individual Christians, churches, and religious institutions to retain their right to freely exercise their religion. For some institutions, this will mean enforcing behavioral codes and leadership and membership standards that align with Christian orthodoxy. For others, it will mean refusing to rent their facilities for gay weddings.

One word of caution: remember that whatever standards your faith community chooses to adopt, you should be consistent. It is not discrimination for a religious community to practice its deeply held convictions, but let's be consistent in how we practice those convictions. To onlookers, being inconsistent looks a lot like being a hypocrite.

What about the individual baker who is reluctant to bake the cake for a gay wedding? We know many Christians who say, "Bake the cake or get out of the business!" But this response trivializes religious freedom. Withholding services from gay customers is not what this debate is about, even if that's how some would portray it. No, this is about preserving a religious person's right not to personally participate in or contribute to an event, such as a gay wedding, that violates their conscience. Some good faith Christians believe doing so affirms such a union, and they cannot play a part without defying their deeply held beliefs. To some, this may seem discriminatory, and of course it raises all sorts of legal questions. But if we want to sort out the religious freedom debate in America, it is critical that we understand, respect, and accommodate individual freedom of conscience, as we explored in earlier chapters.

On the other hand, plenty of Christian bakers (and florists and other wedding service providers) find their contribution to a gay wedding an extraordinary opportunity to serve and build relationships with people. They also wonder if serving gay people could help to repair the Christian community's reputation as antihomosexual.

Engagement in the public square, then, should (and does) reflect a variety of ways God is calling his people to be faithful.

* * *

We hope these five lenses help Christians more clearly see opportunities to live in good faith. As more people interact with this framework, we consistently hear an encouraging sentiment: "This is one of the clearest ways of thinking about this conversation I've ever heard! I don't have to choose love of neighbor over my theology. Both can coexist and *must* coexist for me to be faithful."

That's good faith.

Like them, we hope you are encouraged to know you don't have to be anti-gay to hold tight to your theology. No matter your opinion on what makes for good sexual ethics, we can all agree that we need to do better. We must not walk away from these difficult conversations; we must enter them with grace and truth. We need to recognize that good Christians will disagree about *how* to be compassionate and loving to those with whom we disagree. But for the sake of the gospel and of those who feel abandoned and unwelcome, we can all agree that compassion and love are nonnegotiable.

PART III

THE CHURCH AND OUR FUTURE

16

FIRM CENTER, SOFT EDGES

Good faith Christians are
grounded in Scripture and practice
the art of seeing people.

The setting for the interview was unreal: a beautiful resort near San Diego, California. Seagulls circled in a cloudless sky over the Del Mar tidal region. I showed up to prerecord a segment for a CNN special report on the rise of atheism in the United States; they had asked me to contribute some of Barna's findings on the subject. The segment was slated to be filmed in the office of Deepak Chopra, a well-known New Age spiritualist who rose to fame via frequent stops on *The Oprah Winfrey Show*.

Among the topics on the agenda: whether America is becoming more atheistic and the alleged large number of pastors who are closet atheists.

"The number of people claiming no religion has grown," I told the interviewer. "That means there are more secular Americans today than there were a decade ago. But actually the number of atheists is about the same. Instead, people tend to call themselves agnostics or religiously unaffiliated."

"So what would you say to those who say that secularism is one of the fastest-growing groups in America?"

"America is definitely less Christian than it was twenty-five years ago. And the increasing visibility of atheism is part of that. Yet a lot of the change we are seeing is because researchers are asking the questions differently than they did in the past. When you give people a chance to mark 'not affiliated' or 'none' but you've never offered that option in the past, you don't have any way of tracking a hypothetical increase."

"Do you have evidence that there are some pastors who secretly admit they don't believe in God?"

"No, we don't have any research on that. I am sure you can find someone to interview, but I doubt it's a very large group. Being a pastor is a tough job, but in our research, we don't have a lot of evidence that there is any sort of notable crisis of faith among clergy."

The interview went on for an hour.

About halfway through the taping, the interviewer, Kyra, stopped the cameras to welcome the office owner to the room. Deepak Chopra was here.

"I'm sorry, Deeps. We are running late for your interview." Clearly, Mr. Chopra and Kyra were acquainted.

"No problem. I have an eternity."

* * *

That day in Chopra's office could be seen as a microcosm of faith in our society: a strange mix of Christianity, secularism, and other faith systems trying to find enough common ground to talk about what's happening. But it was also more. That room in San Diego played host to three people created in God's image who had brought their unique needs, desires, and baggage to a conversation about the world.

We are big fans of data, but every day we try to keep in mind that the numbers we toss around represent real people. When we dig into a new data set, the challenge is not only to identify trends in the population but also to see the people in the population.

We want to challenge you to do the same.

If we are going to successfully demonstrate good faith, we must not only understand societal dynamics but also know how to relate them to real people. As we explore the big-picture dimensions of secularism and pluralism in our society, think about people you know (or should get to know) who are atheists, agnostics, and religiously unaffiliated or who profess another faith.

Do you know their story? Are you familiar with the unique needs, desires, and baggage they bring to a conversation? Or are they lumped together in your mind as one big "them"?

Let's take a hard look at the data, but let's also keep in mind who the data represents. Charts, graphs, and tables are helpful, but only as much as they help us see people.

As David reminded the CNN interviewer that day in San Diego, the vast majority of Americans are informed by faith in some way, and Christianity is far and away the dominant player on the US religious scene (as it has been for 350 years or so, once the European population overtook Native Americans). With simple population projections, we can reasonably say that Christianity will continue to be the dominant—but *less* dominant—demographic force in the United States even a hundred years from now.

Christianity holds such massive sway that even now about half the population believes America is best defined as "a Christian nation" (see the table on the following page).

But the signs of a more active secularism are hard to miss. Most people perceive that culture is adrift from its Christian moorings. Four out of five Americans agree with the statement "US society is becoming more secular, meaning more likely to exclude faith and religion from public life." Also, 43 percent of all adults and 57 percent of practicing Christians say the description "a secular nation" fits today's America. Other adults are apt to call the nation "godless" (23 percent) or "post-Christian" (31 percent).

In reality, atheists, agnostics, and the religiously unaffiliated account for only about one-quarter of the population. Their proportion is growing, especially among Millennials, but they are still a minority in the United States.

Common ground is also easy to find.

Even amid a diversity of faith views, there is unity around a couple of big ideas. About one-third of both practicing Christians and non-Christians describe America as "a religiously plural nation" and more than half call it a "nation in transition spiritually." Now, that's something we can agree on.

The perception that we live in a religiously diverse society has some truth, but only about one-tenth of the nation adheres to a faith other than Christianity or secularism. These visions of reality compete and drive much of the religious and ideological conflict we see in public life.

The Best Descriptions of the US Today		

The following is a list of words or phrases. Please indicate whether each is an accurate or not accurate description of the US today.

% "accurate"		
	All Adults	Practicing Christians
A religiously plural nation	66	71
A nation in transition spiritually	53	57
A Christian nation	49	49
A secular nation	43	57
A post-Christian nation	31	39
A godless nation	23	36

Source: Barna OmniPoll, August 2015, *N* = 1,000

Behind the Numbers

There is no question that secularism has momentum in Western society. And as our nation becomes more pluralistic—where all ideas have an equal place at the societal table—we need to understand what opportunities and threats exist for good faith to advance.

When we get behind the big-picture data of opinions and affiliation, there are three underlying realities. And if we can zoom in to see the people, we can respond with care and sophistication as good faith Christians in the days ahead.

The Decline of Legacy Christians

As the following table shows, the number of people who identify themselves as Christians is declining. Nearly 9 out of 10 Elders and Boomers self-describe as Christian, but that number drops to 78 percent among Gen-Xers and just 67 percent among Millennials.

However, our data show the drop-off is happening mostly among legacy Christians, those who self-identify as Christian but don't prioritize faith. The proportion of *practicing* Christians—those who attend worship services monthly and say faith is very important to their lives—is relatively stable. For example, 45 percent of Boomers who self-identify as Christian are practicing, compared to 42 percent of Gen-Xers and 36 percent of Millennials. There's a generational dip, but overall it is much less pronounced. Millennials do face challenges retaining their faith, but among those who do, commitments to the Bible, the church, and Christ are strong.

This is encouraging. While there may be an overall decline in the number of Americans who identify as Christian, the core number of them who prioritize their faithful way of life remains steady and strong. And these believers represent the future of Christianity in America.

The Faith Profile of US Adults				
	% Elders	% Boomers	% Gen-Xers	% Millennials
Self-identified Christians	88	85	78	67
Self-identified atheists, agnostics, or "none"	6	8	13	21
Adherents to faiths other than Christianity	6	6	8	11

Source: Barna *Cities and States* Database, 2009–15, $N = 30,535$
Totals may not equal 100% due to rounding.

We can acknowledge that it's not a bad thing to see superficial forms of faith fade away. When inert faith evaporates, there is greater opportunity for the faithful to stay on mission. But a few questions we should wrestle with are:

- What practices should we incorporate into the life of believers that can be sustained alongside a secular culture?
- How should our churches prioritize reaching seekers (evangelism) and equipping the saints (discipleship)?
- And how do we pass on a strong, vibrant faith heritage to a new generation?

God doesn't need a popular majority to do his work, but if each successive generation has fewer active disciples, there is more work for fewer to do.

The gospel changes everything, starting with our hearts and then bursting into our homes, neighborhoods, and businesses and through the fabric of complicated everyday life. Dallas Willard, in his book *Knowing Christ Today*, makes the argument that Christians need to reclaim faith that speaks to "the very nature of things."[1] Too often, we let scientists and academics decide what counts as reality while religion is consigned to the soft stuff of commitment, perception, and emotion. But the Holy Spirit transforms us into restorers concerned about much more than the "kid's table" of life's issues.

This is the kind of transformative faith we must live and pass on.

Questions about the Bible's Authority

A second overall trend in secular and pluralistic America that's making an impact on real people's lives is widespread skepticism. This is especially true among younger generations, particularly when it comes to the Bible. For a sizable number who start out as Christians, waning trust in God's Word is where they begin to lose their religion. Yes, the vast majority of American households own a Bible, and millions of people, even non-Christians, revere what they know (or have heard) about its wisdom. Yet through research for the American Bible Society, we have tracked an increasing percentage of Americans who say the Bible is just another book written by men, not the inspired Word of God.

When the Bible goes, so goes good faith. This is a huge threat among the next generation.

Among Elders in the United States (age seventy and older), three out of four believe the Bible to be authoritative, and the ratio of those who are engaged with the Bible to those who are skeptical is 4:1. Among the youngest generation of Americans (Millennials, age eighteen to thirty-one), fewer than half believe the Bible is authoritative, and the ratio of Bible engagement to skepticism is 1:2. And as we explored in chapter 4, Millennial non-Christians are much more likely than older Americans to view the Bible as "just a story" (50 percent), "mythology" (38 percent), or "a fairy tale" (30 percent).

These data reflect a sea change in the way young Americans are approaching the Scriptures. If older generations of non-Christians don't exactly believe the Bible, they generally don't find fault with it. Telling someone "the Bible says so" might communicate persuasively among older Americans, but young adults are much less likely to buy it. The prevailing ethos goes, "Keep your dogma to yourself."

We must take a sober look at these trends because Bible attitudes aren't generally influenced by life stage—that is, they don't shift like other religious behaviors when people advance in age. Taking these trends to their logical conclusion, secularism is likely to accelerate. Why? Because reduced trust in the Bible has the same impact as removing the foundation from under a building. Everything starts to crumble.

Many Christians worry about secularism taking over, but secularism shouldn't be our greatest concern. In other words, secularism's advance is downstream from anemic Bible engagement and thin theological thinking. We understand that some Christians today might disagree, but, as evangelicals, we believe the Bible is the inspired Word of the Creator, true in all it affirms, and utterly necessary for understanding who God is, who we are, and how we are meant to live as his people.

Our submission to Scripture's authority is the basis of good faith.

We must relearn to trust in God's ways, even when they run against the grain of current culture. Doing so will include healthy doses of both intellectual honesty and humility. But it's urgent work that must be done because it underpins the "believe" part of the love-believe-live trifecta of good faith living.

The Journey of the iSoul

A third macro-trend is the emergence of the individual as the center of everything. Original sin created the self-absorption problem, but we seem to be living at the height of it. Comparatively, we live in a very narcissistic era. Whether because of consumerism's tentacles or the instant gratification of digital tools, or some combination of other factors, more people are "all about me"—and this includes Christians. As we showed in chapter 4, there is a tremendous amount of individualism in today's society, and that's reflected in the church too. This individualism impacts the practice of good faith in an increasingly secular context because it robs the Christian community of its ability to be countercultural.

- Eighty-four percent of US adults and 66 percent of practicing Christians agree that the "highest goal for life is to enjoy it as much as possible."
- Ninety-one percent of adults and 76 percent of practicing Christians believe that "the best way to find yourself is to look inside yourself."
- Ninety-seven percent of adults and 91 percent of practicing Christians agree that "you have to be true to yourself."

These are simply mind-blowing statistics. Millions of Christians have grafted New Age dogma onto their spiritual persona. When we peel back the layers, we find that many Christians are using the way of Jesus to pursue the way of self. Lucretius seems to be winning the day.

While we wring our hands about secularism spreading through the culture, a majority of churchgoing Christians have embraced corrupt, me-centered theology. Our discipleship efforts must prophetically respond to the "iSpirit" of the age. We should lead people not only to convert to Jesus but also to de-convert from the religion of self.

Christianity is not iFaith. It's not just for Sunday morning when we feel like it or weeknight Bible study when we don't have anything better to do—and it's certainly not just for making us feel good about ourselves. It is an inward work of the Spirit that turns us outward as Christ's body to God's purposes for the world.

The sooner good faith Christians renounce me-me-me belief, the sooner we can offer others a way out of their own self-centeredness.

This is the church at its best: healing sinners of our self-inflicted wounds so we can become healers too.

This won't be easy. Decoupling from the culture's narrative can happen only when communities of faith adopt a new way of life, one rooted in Scripture. This will, indeed, be counter-cultural. But the Christian faith has a pretty good track record when Christians stick to the basics.

Seeing People

My friend Bill and I drove up the California hillside as the sun was slipping toward the horizon. We were invited to a sneak preview of Oprah Winfrey's television miniseries *Belief*—a sort of *Planet Earth*-style documentary about the spiritual lives of human beings.

About 150 or so people representing different faiths gathered in the semidarkened theater, and then Oprah—*Oprah!*—came out and welcomed everyone to Santa Barbara. After a brief introduction, the screen lit up with stories of Christians, Jews, Hindus, Muslims, and more. The cinematography was incredible; the stories of the men and women, boys and girls, were compelling. Oprah's voice narrated the entire documentary.

The lights flickered on, and we were all given a card with directions to Oprah's home for dinner. As we drove the few miles, Bill and I talked about what we did and didn't like about *Belief*. As it turned out, we had both enjoyed much about the episodes we had just viewed. We also wondered what other Christians, especially evangelicals, would think of the series.

"David, do you think it promotes universalism to show multiple faiths on equal footing?" Bill wondered. "And do we Christians really expect someone to make a program about faith—especially a person like Oprah—*without* showing multiple faiths?"

After all, we are living in a pluralistic world.

We drove through beautiful gates onto a tree-lined, cobble-stoned street, where we were greeted by the valet. Walking onto the main lawn, which was the size of a city park, Bill and I took in the towering redwoods and sparkling pond, whipped into small waves by a soaring fountain at its center.

"I feel weird that I had such a hard time with the positive angle they took on all the different religions," I admitted. "I understand why, theologically, it bothered me. But why was I *personally* bugged to watch it? I felt good when Christianity was shown in a positive light but not when other faiths were."

"Yeah, I know what you mean."

"Still, the whole thing was a noncynical approach to talking about faith, and I feel like I should be able to support that, even if I don't agree with everything. So why am I struggling so much?"

These thoughts kept racing through my head, and I realized what was nagging at me. I'd just experienced a beautiful depiction of pluralism at work. Done with the excellence we've come to expect from Oprah, all faiths were given equal weight. But the basic notion being conveyed was that all faith is good, no matter which one you choose.

This was a *fair* thing but not a *true* one. And while all faiths contribute to a lot of good in the world, not all beliefs can be true. They each have ultimate claims that contradict the others. Not all paths lead to heaven.

Good faith Christians must be wary of these distortions. The message that all faiths are true is pluralism at its worst. Instead of respecting diverse points of view (confident pluralism), this relativizes competing beliefs and suggests none of them are actually true; they are just good ways to become more "spiritual."

At the same time, we need to know how to coexist and be present in environments where these distortions are the order of the day.

As twilight came, we and the other guests were seated at tables under an enormous outdoor veranda, and dinner was served. After a bit, Oprah made the rounds and eventually came to our table. As she answered another guest's question, an image of Oprah as a ten-year-old popped into my head—a little girl longing to do good in the world.

Suddenly, I could *see* her. Not just *Oprah!* No, I could see a woman created in God's image, dearly loved by her Creator, and hungry to know him. Even as I drew my own conclusions on what I thought about her television series, I could *see* her a little more clearly: a woman doing everything she knows to do to help people tap into something deeper, something more spiritual. Although her efforts didn't advance the Christian faith exclusively, I wouldn't be judgmental about it, but instead embrace the opportunity to discuss faith wherever and however it comes up. I would see the best in her work and appreciate how her storytelling and cinematic work of art could be a conversation starter.

When Oprah looked my way, I said, "I spend a lot of time thinking about the spiritual journeys of Millennials . . . why they stay connected to their faith tradition and why they don't. I think one of the strong parts of *Belief* is the sincere way it shows young people, Christians included, finding faith. That's not the norm today; most Millennials lose confidence in their faith. But *Belief* shows that faith traditions matter and can be passed on from one generation to the next."

"Thank you for that," she replied and then described some of the production decisions that led to that emphasis. After a few more minutes of discussion, she thanked us and made her way to another table.

That's when I looked around that luxurious outdoor dining room and *saw* my fellow guests of various faiths: people who are seeking, to whom Jesus has promised if they will pray, "Keep on seeking, and you will find" (Matt. 7:7). My heart leapt at the potential.

When we relate to people who are not Christians, whether secular or of another faith, we have to get the love + believe + live = good faith equation right. As our friend Barry Corey says, Christians should have "soft edges and firm centers."[2] Jesus related to people this way. Think about his interaction with the woman at the well. Or his responses to his interrogators. Or his life-giving answers to those with hungry hearts. He spoke truth from a "firm center," but his hospitable, humble "soft edges" allowed people to get close enough to hear him.

Jesus practiced the sacred art of seeing people.

When we have soft edges and firm centers, we can *see* people Jesus dearly loves. And when, aided by the Holy Spirit, we see them, we can look beyond the trends and into real people's hurts, hopes, and needs.

It's too easy for us to look the other way, isn't it? Gabe once hosted a Muslim imam at a Q Conference, the imam who was responsible for the so-called Ground Zero Mosque that created a stir in New York City and across America. A few months later, Imam Feisal would become his neighbor in Manhattan. For Gabe, extending that invitation was an expression of a soft edge, even as he kept hold of his firm center. And while Gabe made it clear from the stage that he didn't agree with or support the imam's theology, he also expressed how important it is for good faith Christians to hear from a devout Muslim.

Most of the Q attenders were open and receptive; they could see that listening, learning, and seeking to understand are worthwhile. But others felt Gabe was implicitly endorsing this man's perspectives merely by inviting him to be seen and heard. A few of them took to Twitter to voice their disapproval, tweeting their way through the imam's remarks to let the world know how their time was being wasted.

They may have felt that way, but they missed an opportunity to *see.*

Living in a pluralistic culture means learning how to get along, understand the "other," build friendships, and communicate across divides. These are essential skills.

Good faith Christians lead the way when we have confidence in what we believe and practice seeing those who believe differently.

17

CHURCH IN A NEW WORLD

Good faith churches make
disciples who bless the world.

We waited to see how the story would be told in the press.

Last year Barna released the findings of a yearlong research project on the state of faith, Christianity, and the church in Scotland. As part of the release, David did a brief tour of a few major cities in Scotland. At each stop, he engaged in local press interviews on some of the most notable findings—among them, that Christianity is viewed favorably by a majority of Scots and that young adults in Scotland express greater interest in the Bible than their elders.

At first, this seems counterintuitive. Who could explain why young adults were more interested in the Christian scriptures than their parents? Because most indicators point to an overwhelming trend toward secularization in Scotland, the favorable data surprised many people (including Barna researchers). If they chose to report on the study at all, how would this research be interpreted and reported by the local media?

Over the culinary delights of a Scottish breakfast, the tour's publicist, Stephanie, distributed copies of a daily newspaper from the city of Dundee.

"Faith in Scotland Offers Hope to Christian Groups."

The news item recited some of the positive findings and quoted Alan MacWilliam, a minister from Glasgow, who felt encouraged about the research.

Then the article took a turn. The reporter had invited Spencer Fildes, chairman of the Scottish Secular Society, to respond to the research. He was not impressed. He questioned the validity of the findings (the typical response from those who don't like the results). And then he expressed his true feelings.

> People now struggle to associate religion with anything other than conflict, sectarianism, child abuse, homophobia, misogyny, violence and privilege. Religion is now perceived as the catalyst for the horrors we see on our televisions every day. The advent of the internet has led to an explosion of evidence-based understanding, with secularism challenging the status quo and unjustifiable privilege of the Churches.[1]

Wow! He wasn't pulling any punches.

He painted a perfect picture of the two primary perceptions many in the world have of Christians: irrelevant and extreme. Now, if we Christians were to use similar language to describe another group, we would definitely *not* be quoted by the paper of record in Dundee—unless it was to prove once and for all how irrelevant and extreme we are!

This offers us another learning moment.

If Christians were to use similar language about another group, we might deserve whatever payback came our way. Insulting other groups, no matter how off base or "unjustifiably privileged," is not in our love-believe-live job description. Our resolve to love the "other" must supersede our desire to win in the court of public opinion.

Paul wrote to the Christians in Corinth:

> I told you not to associate with people who indulge in sexual sin. But I wasn't talking about unbelievers who indulge in sexual sin, or are greedy, or cheat people, or worship idols. You would have to leave this world to avoid people like that. I meant that you are not to associate with anyone who claims to be a believer yet indulges in sexual sin, or is greedy, or worships idols, or is abusive, or is a drunkard, or cheats people. Don't even eat with such people. It isn't my responsibility to judge outsiders, but it certainly is your responsibility to judge those inside the church who are sinning. (1 Cor. 5:9–12)

Paul was saying there is a big difference between how we engage with the world and how we engage in Christian community. And we would humbly suggest that conflating, confusing, or emphasizing one over the other of these two postures weakens the church inside and out.

When outward engagement is our sole aim, we become moralistic crusaders or proponents of a purely social gospel that has no power to save people from sin. On the other hand, if we focus solely on what happens inside the church, we become pious separatists who are so heavenly minded we are no earthly good for God's plan to renew the world through Christ in his people.

We believe good faith churches are called to hold these two in tandem, to live in the necessary, perpetual tension between knitting together a community of disciples and going out to bless the world.

Facing Outward

In 2010, a University of Pennsylvania professor and a nonreligious research group in Philadelphia decided to see if they could determine the economic "halo effect" of a house of worship on the surrounding community. They wanted to figure out a congregation's economic worth, if any, to the local community it serves.

Using a metric of fifty-four factors, researchers tallied up the economic benefits of ten Protestant churches, one Catholic parish, and one synagogue in Philadelphia.

The grand total for the twelve congregations combined? Over $50 million *every year*.[2]

These startling economic indicators point to a church's worth. And, generally speaking, people's perceptions jibe with the economics. Most think the presence of a church is a favorable thing for a community. Half of US adults say it's "very" and another 30 percent say it's "somewhat" favorable—that's eight out of ten Americans who see churches as beneficial to their surrounding communities.

But favorable in what way?

In a 2014 study commissioned by World Vision, a majority of Australians said they think churches should be involved in the public-square issues of child protection and human rights. They liked the idea of churches contributing to the overall common good. But when the question of church involvement got more personal, people weren't so sure. Only one-quarter said being an active part of a church could help them think through the spiritual side of their lives or enhance friendships and connection with the community—and those were the *most popular* of the options.[3]

In other words, the value of a church is, for many, theoretical rather than personal. Church is good. For other people.

When we asked US adults to identify needs in their community they believe churches could meet, about half pointed to practical, physical needs such as providing food and clothes to those without, or offering shelter for homeless people and activities for teens.

When it comes to spiritually oriented needs, people would like a church to keep things general rather than specifically Christian. About half said a local church could provide "spiritual guidance," "a place where everyone is accepted," or "counseling services," but they were less enthusiastic about "teaching the Bible/teaching people about Jesus" and "instilling morals or values."

People who are not actively engaged in a church often do not consider Bible teaching to be very desirable. They might even consider it irrelevant—like someone teaching a hopelessly complex board game. Yet we know of Christians who have led people to faith in Christ by hosting Bible studies in their homes. We firmly believe the gospel is relevant to all people at all times, even if it seems unpopular at the time.

It is also disarmingly powerful when churches serve their communities in unexpected ways. This is especially true when the perceptions of Christian irrelevance and extremism are thick in the air. Mission Church in Ventura, California, led by David's friends Mike and Jodi Hickerson, is one of dozens of churches around the country that host an annual prom for special-needs teens and young adults called "A Night to Remember." In 2012, the first year of the event, 150 student volunteers dressed in their finest evening attire threw a huge party for 60 special guests, most of whom had never attended a prom or even a dance. All the guests got to pick out their own dresses and corsages, tuxes and boutonnieres, have their hair and makeup done by a professional stylist, and then take a limo ride with their student host before walking (or rolling, in the case of kids cruising in wheelchairs) the red carpet.

Amanda, an eighteen-year-old prom guest, had watched her three older sisters experience the prom rite of passage, but Amanda and her mom, Mary, never dreamed she would also get to experience it. Mary said, "I just think it was really great for Mission Church to recognize a need and reach out to the community. . . . There are so many things people with special needs will never be able to realize. This is not something everyone gets to do."[4]

Paul calls believers "Christ's ambassadors" who have been given the "task of reconciling people to him" (see 2 Cor. 5:18–20). But effective ambassadors don't train themselves. They mature when they live life in Christian community, discipled to love and care for those Christ loved so much.

One of the jobs of an ambassador is to throw lavish parties that bring people together to experience the generosity of the host nation—which in our case is the kingdom of God. So it's not hard to argue that "A Night to Remember" is perfectly in line with the church's mission to share God's "wonderful message of reconciliation" (v. 19).

Maybe you recall the story Jesus tells recorded in Matthew 22. He says the kingdom of God is like a big party that includes the people no one else would think to invite. Just imagine how Jesus must feel about the modern embodiment of his parable.

But attending big parties isn't the only way people should encounter the gospel. We are commanded to tell people the good news about Jesus. This should, of course, be demonstrated in our lives but must also be proclaimed with words.

As we pointed out in chapter 3, 60 percent of adults believe it is "extreme" to share your faith with others. That's why we must relearn the sacred art of meaningful, spiritual conversations that point people to Jesus. Without a costly investment in relationship combined with boldness to speak up, people may never hear about the opportunity to become a new creation in Christ.

Our friend Jon Tyson, pastor of Trinity Grace Church in New York City, coaches Trinity's people for evangelism. He emphasizes forming no-agenda relationships with others; walking up to strangers and proclaiming your beliefs might catalyze a new thought, but the long, hard work of relationships is more likely to produce a transformational result.

Then Jon encourages his congregation to recognize two key times when friends, family members, and colleagues are most open to being introduced to Jesus. First, a season of personal crisis. This could be a divorce, the loss of a family member, a bankruptcy, a major career shift, or even the loneliness of moving to the "big city." Second, a moment of national or global tragedy. Whether a terrorist attack like 9/11, Hurricane Katrina, the Syrian refugee crisis, an earthquake in Nepal or

Argentina, or the church shooting in Charleston, South Carolina—when a man-made tragedy or a natural disaster strikes, our hearts pause to contemplate deeper questions about life and what it all means. So often, these are the times when Christ's knocking on the heart's door is louder than a person's indifference (see Rev. 3).

When we invest in relationships, trust God to bring opportunities, and then boldly share what the Spirit puts in our heart—we can proclaim Jesus as Lord in a way people can hear and respond to.

Whether it's throwing a prom for special-needs teens, providing practical and relational resources for homeless people, caring for children whose parents are struggling financially or emotionally, hosting weekend camps so high school students can hear the truth about Jesus, coaching immigrant students in English literacy, bringing diverse leaders together to stem the tide of racism in our communities, sharing our personal stories of salvation with friends and neighbors, supporting moms-to-be who don't have a husband or sharing our personal stories of salvation with friends and neighbors—these and countless others are the reconciling, proclaiming, restorative, outward-facing activities of a good faith church.

When communities of good faith nurture relationships with and serve alongside people whom God loves, it's more likely that good faith Christians will have the opportunity to follow the apostle Peter's instructions: "If someone asks about your hope as a believer, always be ready to explain it. But do this in a gentle and respectful way" (1 Pet. 3:15–16). Because, of course, sharing the gospel is one of the most important outward-facing activities Christians do.

Growing Inward

To be good faith Christians, we need to engage the world around us. But to do that, we must cultivate the health of our churches and our souls. The early church is described as devoted to "the apostles' teaching, and to fellowship, and to sharing in meals (including the Lord's Supper), and to prayer" (Acts 2:42). Without robust attention to internal growth—both inside each believer (growing as a disciple) and among the church as a whole (growing as Christ's body)—Christians are merely do-gooders lacking the power that comes from being transformed by the Holy Spirit.

Jesus gave his followers the Great Commission *as a community*, not as a solo project. Making disciples, while surely a mission each believer is called to, is primarily the task of the church. To most Christians, the process of spiritual growth that we commonly call "discipleship" is best defined as "becoming more like Christ."[5] And, as even a cursory look at Jesus's life reveals, being like Christ has both an inward and an outward component.

But how does discipleship actually work? How do communities of faith help people become the kind of disciples who grow in good faith for the sake of the world?

Our work in Scotland provides a few insights. One element of the project was to assess what qualities or priorities distinguish growing churches from those churches that are maintaining or declining in attendance. What are the best practices of growing churches in a post-Christian context?

We found nine factors that make a significant difference between baseline churches (maintaining or declining) and growing churches. These factors impact church health in an increasingly secular culture. Among these nine, four are external pursuits:

1. Prioritizing outreach by serving the poor and sharing faith
2. Partnering with other churches and causes
3. Being innovative for the sake of the gospel
4. Focusing on receptive teens and young adults

And four factors are internal goals:

5. Teaching the Bible thoroughly
6. Fostering close Christian community
7. Developing new leaders
8. Leading with a team that has diverse skills and spiritual gifts

The ninth factor, praying, is both inward looking (spiritual practice) and outward facing (mission). In the growing churches, members and leaders were two to three times more likely to say they "pray specifically for living faithfully in a post-Christian culture." Even though the two groups of churches were comprised of people who believe similar things theologically, a major difference emerged in how they *practice* prayer. Growing churches pray missionally and make prayer a mission.

Here's another important difference. Among growing churches in Scotland, more than nine out of ten pastors say they teach the Bible using a systematic, or expository, approach. Among baseline churches, only about one-third of pastors approach Bible teaching this way. This is an enormous disparity and, we believe, indicates that immersion in Scripture is a driver of church growth and spiritual vitality. The difference is not just following a "successful" teaching formula, but challenging congregants to learn and wrestle with the Scriptures.

Of course no church is perfect. But overall, good faith Christians and churches are thriving in post-Christian Scotland—and should serve as an example to us. Growing inward with Christ and facing outward as the body of Christ is a powerful combination. These churches and their leaders seem to be getting the love + believe + live equation right, and it's having an effect on a new generation.

Which brings us to the role of pastors.

Christian Leaders as Teachers to the World

Pastors play a vital role in the shaping of good faith, but it is not easy. In his book *Knowing Christ Today*, Dallas Willard identifies some of the cultural pressures on pastors. The book, first published in 2009, seems to anticipate some of the extremist and irrelevant perceptions with which we now contend. While admitting these pressures are real and difficult, Willard gives pastors a broader vision of their role than many typically envision. He writes persuasively that pastors must rethink their position in society:

> The task of Christian pastors and leaders is to present Christ's answers to the basic questions of life and to bring those answers forward *as* knowledge—primarily to those who are seeking and are open to following him, but also to all who happen to hear, in the public arenas of a world in desperate need of knowledge of what is real and good. . . .
>
> [Pastors] have an audience—an audience of people spread, to a greater or lesser degree, throughout the community—and their position in the world as God's spokespeople is unique. They deal, if they will, with the questions that frame human worldviews. Answers to those questions provide the

orientations of individual lives and whole societies. For good or ill, they determine the essential character of all we do, whether we are conscious of them or not.[6]

Good faith, indeed.

Pastors are ambassadors and guides to the good faith way of life, and many are doing their very best to fill that role. Still, these complicated, uncertain times require an even greater degree of clarity, courage, and tender shepherding from today's pastors and priests.

We are reminded of Paul's admonition to the church in Corinth where he says, "I am not writing these things to shame you, but to warn you as my beloved children. For even if you had ten thousand others to teach you about Christ, you have only one spiritual father. For I became your father in Christ Jesus when I preached the Good News to you" (1 Cor. 4:14–15).

A major challenge in the American church today is our elevation of the teaching gift. Many pastors of the largest churches, bestselling authors, and generally accepted "leaders" of the American church are teachers, not spiritual fathers and mothers. While video venue churches and podcast learning continue to trend in some communities, the deficit of "fathering" is being felt in a new generation. Confused disciples don't do much good in a broken world. We will always need good teaching, but pastors who are loving parents may be the need of the hour as cultural change continues at breakneck speed.

Let's acknowledge that it's a difficult time to be a church leader. For one thing, pastors are vastly outnumbered: the ratio of senior Christian clergy to all other Americans, including minors, is 1 to 963. And, for many, a life of vocational ministry is no walk in the park. According to research Barna conducted for Pepperdine University, about half of US pastors say ministry has been hard on their family, and three out of ten say ministry has been a personal disappointment. Nearly half report struggling with depression, one-quarter with significant marital problems or parenting difficulties, and about one out of six with an addiction of some kind.[7]

Correlation is not causation, so it's an open question what impact these personal struggles have on ministry effectiveness. Regardless of the causes, however, we can identify the beginnings of a leadership crisis in US churches.

One indicator is that many pastors are reluctant to teach about certain topics for fear of negative reactions. In a study among US clergy, 40 percent of Protestant pastors and more than half of Catholic priests told us they "frequently" or "occasionally" feel limited in their ability to speak about moral and social issues out of concern that people will take offense. And among these leaders, two-thirds report greater concern about their parishioners' reactions than about the response of people outside their congregation.

It is a tall order to communicate with truth and grace in today's polarized world, but if pastors are editing their words for fear of offending their people, this is cause for great concern.

In the long run, their reluctance will do the church no favors. Columnist Rod Dreher recently wrote:

> No church can be the church if its pastors and its congregation are unwilling to speak hard truths to each other and to themselves. To think of the pastorate as primarily a "helping profession," and church as chiefly a therapeutic community, in the sense of guiding us to feel better about ourselves, as opposed to giving us what we need to be healed, is a betrayal of the Gospel and the church's mission.[8]

Sharp words, but he's right. The old adage "Comfort the afflicted and afflict the comfortable" is a decent summary of the prophetic authority inherent in a pastoral calling. The hard part, of course, is keeping the contours of orthodoxy intact while caring for the most vulnerable in our faith communities. College leaders, youth pastors, and mentors working with teens and young adults may find this especially challenging. Young people who experience same-sex attraction, for instance, need to know God loves and accepts them just as they are and, *at the same time*, need wise counsel and practical tools for fruitful living within God's intention for human sexuality.

Tricky, right? But trickiness does not give leaders a pass.

Perhaps we need to be reminded, bombarded as we are by leadership strategies and church-growth tactics, that God's definition of ministry success is nothing more and nothing less than faithfulness and fruitfulness. These go hand in hand. If we've got one without the other—say, if weekly financial giving has increased (fruitfulness) but we're pulling punches in the pulpit (lack of faithfulness)—it's time to do some serious self-reflection. Maybe Psalm 139 could be of help: "Search me, O God, and know my heart; test me and know my anxious thoughts. Point out anything in me that offends you, and lead me along the path of everlasting life" (vv. 23–24).

The Church as a Counterculture

Pastors play an essential role helping to fine-tune a church's balance of discipleship and cultural engagement, the inside-outside dynamic we've been exploring in this chapter. The church sets itself apart as a counterculture by devoting sustained energy to both inward and outward expressions of discipleship. When Peter wrote to the persecuted Christians in Asia, whom he called "temporary residents and foreigners," he sketched the broad outlines:

> You are a chosen people. You are royal priests, a holy nation, God's very own possession. As a result, you can show others the goodness of God, for he called you out of the darkness into his wonderful light. "Once you had no identity as a people; now you are God's people. Once you received no mercy; now you have received God's mercy." (1 Pet. 2:9–10)

These first-century believers could bless the world by showing God's goodness because they had answered God's call to become a holy nation, a new community living in God's light and shining in the darkness.

St. Augustine explored the idea further in his fifth-century classic, *The City of God*. His goal was to reassure Christians who were freaking out about the sack of Rome by the Goths. He reminded them that they were citizens of a City, the New Jerusalem, which could not be overcome even by marauding barbarians. The world as they knew it was falling down around their ears, but Augustine encouraged them to look beyond the borders of Rome to the new nation God was building in the church: "This heavenly city, while it sojourns on earth, calls citizens out of all nations, and gathers together a society of pilgrims of all languages."[9]

The heavenly city has its own distinctive culture, which often contradicts, or counters, the broader culture. In an essay aptly titled "The Church as Culture," theologian Robert Louis Wilken writes, "The Church is a culture in its own right. Christ does not simply infiltrate a culture; Christ creates culture by forming another city, another sovereignty with its own social and political life."[10]

How can we do this?

There are many ways.

First, our commitment to Christ revealed in the Scriptures, and our submission to the Spirit's authority in our lives and churches, mark us as children of the Father. We seek God's will instead of our personal fulfillment, in direct contrast to the surrounding culture.

Second, our commitment to one another, our unity, forming households, practicing hospitality, being faithful in our marriages, and sharing grace with our neighbors are just a few of the ways our counterculture stands in contrast to the wider world.

Third, we can live in countercultural rhythms. We can practice the Sabbath, determined to take one day each week to rest and remind ourselves, and our colleagues and neighbors, that our value doesn't come from what we produce. It is found in whose we are.

A fourth area is how we manage our technology—how we think about and use our digital devices. Let's be the best at putting down our technology, setting aside distractions, and focusing on real people. Turn your phone off when entering into a coffee shop conversation with a friend. Be determinedly "present" when engaging with your family.[11]

Fifth is the issue of stewardship: using our talents, passions, and work life as gifts from God to serve others. God has a special and unique calling for every person to do good in his world. "We are God's masterpiece. He has created us anew in Christ Jesus, so we can do the good things he planned for us long ago" (Eph. 2:10). Vocational discipleship—learning to be faithful in answer to God's call—is a perfect example of inward development for outward focus. Good faith Christians understand vocation as a dynamic between an inward cultivation of our hearts and an outward expression of our faith in the world.

These are a few ways every good faith Christian can practice countercultural living. But parents especially need to get in the game.

Being a Countercultural Parent

As the dominant culture's influence grows, our children and their children have little hope of holding firm to a faith distorted by society's corrupt moral code. And so, as in centuries past, Christians should be intentional about forming communities and institutions (churches, schools, networks) that remain at a distance from mainstream culture. Environments that emphasize holiness as a part of good faith will help create a new generation of disciples with deep-rooted faith.

We are not suggesting that Christians should remove themselves entirely from the world or that every Christian child should go to a Christian school. We *are* saying that families, schools, households, and churches will need to be spaces where holy and righteous living are modeled, practiced, and taught in order to prepare our children to follow Jesus and engage the wider world.

We are both parents to boys and girls who are preteens and teens, and we know firsthand how tough it is to be a good faith parent in a culture that constantly pulls our children into an alternate reality. Based on everything we've been learning as researchers and leaders and everything we're experiencing as parents, we are convinced that we must get the inside-outside tension right as we raise our kids.

We make it a habit to talk about everything from sex to Taylor Swift lyrics with our kids. Recent months have seen conversations about the money we make (and give away), the reasons modesty is important, how God uses human beauty for his good, and how he sometimes uses our brokenness more than our strengths. As our kids consider college and future careers or hobbies, we chat about how these are expressions of God's calling in their lives. We have candid conversations about our own dreams and foibles too—working too much, taking ourselves too seriously, and more. (And of course there are lighter-fare topics like sports, friends, and smoothies.)

David's kids regularly point out that he is more likely than they are to spend a digital moment on Twitter or email, so we don't want to sound like we're getting it 100 percent right.

Still, if equipping people to have difficult conversations is a big hope for this book, that has to include conversations not only with the non-Christians we know but also at home with our families.

If we focus on only the inward spiritual development of our children, we will fail to prepare them to be on a mission for Jesus in their generation. These young people may have strong faith, but faith is not *Christian* if it fails to be effectively expressed *in the world*. Conversely, if we over-focus on preparation for life in today's complex culture without attending to a deep understanding and practice of holiness, we risk their identity becoming innately *of the world*.

This is Jesus's prayer for his disciples recorded in John 17: that we might be in the world but not of the world. Growing inward and facing outward.

18

FAITHFUL IN EXILE

Good faith Christians *love* their
neighbors, *believe* in God's power at
work in his people, and *live* into God's
call to be agents of reconciliation.

"It's like we're living in a modern-day Babylon."

I recently overheard two Christian friends discussing today's seemingly out-of-control culture. One of the guys felt like an ancient pagan civilization was the closest analogy he could find.

And his friend immediately agreed. "Definitely!"

Babylon.

Why would Christians reference an ancient culture to describe today's society? If you had to describe mainstream culture in a single word or phrase, what would you choose?

Complicated.

Accelerated.

Complex.

Pleasure-seeking and narcissistic.

Spiritual but godless.

Strong and powerful yet corrupt and immoral.

Confused about right and wrong.

In ancient times, Babylon was an empire that, like empires before and since, overwhelmed other lands and peoples with military and commercial power and sought to obliterate competing cultures. In the seventh-century BC, the king of Babylon, Nebuchadnezzar, laid siege to Jerusalem, and the kingdom of Judah fell to the empire. To complete Babylon's dominance of Judah, Nebuchadnezzar took captive most of the noble families, craftsmen, artisans, soldiers, and other prominent citizens, carting them all off to the empire's capital.

One Hebrew, in particular, stood out.

Daniel, a member of a Judean noble family, was human plunder of a military conquest, a victim of human trafficking. He came from the ethnically and religiously homogenous culture of Judah and was taken by force to the cosmopolitan and religiously plural capital. It was something like *The Hunger Games*, if you think about it. All the "districts" of the Babylonian Empire were coerced into sending their best and brightest to serve the interests of the capital.

It's not hard to imagine that Daniel and others who were taken captive felt outnumbered, dislocated, and culturally out of step—the very feelings many Christians and other believers are experiencing today.

We believe our faith community today faces an emerging social context that demands we learn to be Christian in a new way, described best as being "faithful in exile." We are no longer the home team, even though our physical location hasn't changed. We're playing on Babylon's turf.

A Call to Hope

Exile. Many people think this is a depressing prognosis for the church. Yet in the last few years, in doing public talks on this topic, we've found that it resonates with many Christians. The idea that we are in a new age—a modern-day Babylon—especially connects with pastors, parents, and grandparents who are trying to understand the kind of culture that is forming the next generation.

We need an accurate handle to describe living in today's culture. While to some this description may seem over the top, exile fits what many Christians are experiencing.

As people of good faith, we hope for the world one day to come but must describe the world as it is today. As Max DePree says, "The first responsibility of the leader is to define reality."[1] Leaders in the church today need to understand our times in order to shape a God-oriented future. We think the phrases "modern-day Babylon" and "digital Babylon" effectively describe today's complex systems of human-centered activity. And the idea of exile aptly describes what faithful Christian living looks like under this regime.

Maybe the idea of exile works for you. Maybe it doesn't. You may wonder, when we use the metaphor of exile, if the two of us have simply given up hope.

No. Exactly the opposite!

We could not be more hopeful about the future of the Christian community, even in this most complicated and accelerated of contexts.

Embracing the exile metaphor means we retain at least two important theological views: that God is sovereign and that God has plans for his people. According to the biblical writings on exile, God uses exile to purify his people and reorient them toward his purposes.

As Christians, we believe God knows what he is doing and is not surprised or confounded by ungodly civilizations. Daniel, perhaps the Bible's most famous exile, says as much to King Nebuchadnezzar in Daniel 4: "The Most High rules over the kingdoms of the world. He gives them to anyone he chooses" (v. 17). When we maintain the belief that God knows where all this is headed—toward his ends and purposes—we don't have to worry about the direction of culture. We just need to be faithful to God and to his calling.

In exile, we learn to trust God.

Good Faith in Exile

Let's take a look at three lessons we can learn from Daniel and other biblical exiles. They show us that being faithful in exile means providing a prophetic, countercultural response to the spirit of the age.

Love: The Power of Actions, Language, and Respect

What we do and say matters—and *how* we act and speak matters too.

We have attempted to weave this theme throughout *Good Faith*. Aggressors tend to lose. When Houston's lesbian mayor subpoenaed the sermons and correspondence of five local pastors who opposed the city's bill expanding public access to transgender men and women—including to restrooms—the backlash was immediate. Many people on both sides of the political aisle concluded the subpoenas were "intended to intimidate and to bully pastors into silence," and the mayor was forced to withdraw them.[2]

There is a world of difference between confidently asserting what we believe and being aggressive in faith-driven "beast mode." There will be times when Christians are essentially minding our own business and are swept up into some larger public debate or quarrel. That's what happened to Gordon College, an evangelical institution of higher learning north of Boston. The college's accreditor, the New England Association of Schools and Colleges, threatened to withdraw accreditation unless the administration adopted a position and policies related to homosexuality that would violate its values and mission.

Gordon College didn't go looking for a fight. But when the fight came to them, they responded with confidence in Christian orthodoxy while acting and speaking with respect for their opposition. And in the end, the NEASC relented and religious liberty won the day.[3]

Regardless of the circumstances, the principle is clear: *what* we do and say and *how* we do and say it are all critical to good faith.

Daniel understood this.

When King Nebuchadnezzar demanded that someone interpret his nightmares, all the pagan philosophers chickened out—and for their cowardice earned themselves a death sentence. Daniel, however, advocated for their lives to be spared. And then, in one of the most famous biblical examples of good faith speaking truth to power, Daniel told King Neb the meaning of his dream: he was about to lose it all. The next in a long line of empires, Persia, was on its way to bring him down.

The prophet was confident and assertive but delivered the bad news with utmost respect.

Whatever you think of Pope Francis, his actions and words of respect for all sorts of people have had a measurable impact on perceptions of the Catholic Church. When he greets children or those who are disabled or disfigured—who are often last to receive society's respect—his face glows with delight. His commitment to the core doctrines of Christian orthodoxy seem to be unchanged, but Francis's words and deeds shine with good faith.

Jesus's ministry offers one lesson after another on the importance of acting and speaking with respect. His Sermon on the Mount could (and probably should) be our textbook in this regard. Jesus says, "Blessed are the peacemakers, for they will be called children of God" (Matt. 5:9 NIV). He's not talking about mere peacekeeping, like being an impartial referee who breaks up a hockey fight. He's saying people of good faith should *make* peace. Doing so requires words, actions, and respect.

When he says to "go the extra mile"—one of many Jesus phrases still in the modern lexicon—he is talking about a countercultural act of respectful service.

When he goes to Zacchaeus's house, he acts with undeserved respect toward the tax collector and social pariah.

When he reminds the woman at the well about her many illicit relationships, he speaks truth with respect, not with condescension or insult.

Acting and speaking with respect demonstrate our love for people and for the God who created them.

Believe: The Power of God

A second lesson we can learn from Daniel is how to act on our beliefs in a hostile culture. It is our firm conviction that orthodox Christianity is relevant to all people in all times. But how can we hold these beliefs in an increasingly pagan culture? Daniel's unwavering commitment to God, his active prayer life, and his desire to see God work in miraculous ways are examples to us.

In Daniel 9, the aging exile prophet writes about the influence of Jeremiah on his faithfulness. He says he has been reading the scrolls of Jeremiah, and we might presume to imagine he has in mind Jeremiah's remarkable instructions, written nearly one hundred years before, to those who would be caught up in the coming exile:

> This is what the LORD of Heaven's Armies, the God of Israel, says to all the captives he has exiled to Babylon from Jerusalem: "Build homes, and plan to stay. Plant gardens, and eat the food they produce. Marry and have children. Then find spouses for them so that you may have many grandchildren. Multiply! Do not dwindle away! And work for the peace and prosperity of the city where I sent you into exile. Pray to the LORD for it, for its welfare will determine your welfare." (Jer. 29:4–7)

Jeremiah's predictions came true. Daniel and his peers were now under the power of a cosmopolitan, godless society. And these young Hebrews had to make sense of and live faithfully in a culture that didn't just decimate its enemies; it brainwashed them too. Babylon's brutal education was a form of moral and spiritual imperialism; their "training methods" were designed such that the empire's worldview would take root in the hearts and minds of its captives.

In spite of this totalizing imperial strategy, the most remarkable story of faithfulness in exile emerges: these young men routinely stood up for their faith, putting their lives on the line when threatened with flames and ravenous lions.

Their belief was steadfast. And God honored their faithfulness.

His supernatural power intervened on behalf of Shadrach, Meshach, and Abednego when they were thrown into the fire for refusing to worship the king. His supernatural power safeguarded Daniel in the lions' den when he was sentenced to death for praying to the one true God.

We aren't responsible for the outcome, but we are responsible to be faithful.

When God's people trust the biblical witness and are faithful to Christian practice, God brings his power to life in them. He may not always save us from the fiery furnace (or the militant's sword), but his power will manifest itself in ways that cannot be denied, even by those who oppose him.

Live: The Power of Vocation

The final lesson we learn from Daniel relates to following the call of God on our lives. It's unlikely we would know about Daniel at all if he had not pursued his vocation. He essentially became the secretary of state for one of the most pagan civilizations in human history. He served at the pleasure of three kings, leaders of a triad of ungodly regimes that rose to power in quick succession.

Our love and orthodoxy bring good to society when we pursue our God-given calling. This includes our career—entrepreneurs, public officials, scientists, writers, teachers, pastors, dental hygienists, and so on. But it also encompasses how we parent, how we practice hospitality, how we steward our sexual lives, and how we engage in conversations. We are called to be faithful in all of life's complexities. Our love and belief should compel us to become agents of God's reconciliation through Christ in whatever sphere of life he has called us to inhabit.

Jeremiah's how-to-survive-in-exile instructions are as applicable today as they were thousands of years ago: plant gardens, build houses, and plan to stay. Work for your city's peace and prosperity, for its flourishing will be your flourishing. As a community of God, work for the common good: that which is orderly and right, abundant and generous, beautiful and flourishing with life and relationships.

Hopeful expectation in exile is a biblical perspective. Not only do we have examples of actual exiles like Joseph, Esther, and Daniel, but much of the New Testament also calls us to live "in the world but not of the world." Peter says we are sojourners, strangers in the world. Paul and the writer of Hebrews offer practical wisdom for fine-tuning the church's role in relation to the wider culture. "Bless those who persecute you," Paul writes. "Don't curse them; pray that God will bless them. . . . Live in harmony with each other" (Rom. 12:14, 16). "Work at living in peace with everyone," Hebrews says, "and work at living a holy life" (12:14).

This is the argument we have done our best to make in *Good Faith.*

The Christian community is called to be a counterculture for the common good. We are countercultural when we:

love others well
remain committed to orthodox beliefs
make space for those who disagree

stand out from the crowd

ask the right questions

live under God's moral order

offer a vision of human intimacy beyond sex

practice hospitality

do the good, hard work of racial reconciliation

value human life in every form, at every stage

love our gay friends and trust God's design for sex

build households of faith

are theologically grounded and culturally responsive

make disciples

practice the sacred art of seeing people

make disciples and faith communities that are Christlike

We have a lot of work to do. At times, you may feel irrelevant or be labeled extreme. But you are in good company. Through the ages, the Christian community has faced pressure—even persecution—and endured.

We are called not to determine the outcome but to be faithful.

Led by love, grounded in biblical belief, and ready to live as a counterculture for the common good, we trust that our good faith will be used by God to renew the world.

ACKNOWLEDGMENTS

If it had depended solely on us, this project wouldn't have seen the light of day. There are so many colleagues, friends, and mentors we want to thank for their contributions to *Good Faith*.

Our partner and editor on this project, Aly Hawkins, was the glue that held the writing process together. Like a great navigator, she steered us clear of trouble and ensured our writing journey would reach its ultimate destination. It's not easy pulling these two voices into one, but you did it beautifully. Thank you for your wisdom, posture, and gift with words—we are so grateful for you.

A special thanks to our friend Chris Ferebee. Pulling a project like this together was no small task. Thanks for carrying the load. You make the entire process enjoyable and allow us to do what we do best.

Jack Kuhatschek, your patience, prudence, and long-suffering over the past year have been phenomenal. Thanks for helping us refine the vision for this book and for extending deadlines so we could create it. Thanks also to Dave Lewis, Mark Rice, and Dwight Baker for championing this project.

To those who contributed feedback along the way and gave inspiration and insights, thank you: David Bailey, David and Jason Benham, Cory Maxwell-Coghlan, Jim Henderson, Reggie Joiner, Gary Kinnaman, Steve McBeth, Carey Neiuwhof, Kara Powell, Megan Pritchett, Julie Rodgers, Preston Sprinkle, Roxanne Stone, and Michael Wear helped to round out the rough edges and articulate why this book matters for today's Christians.

Pat MacMillan, thank you for the encouragement to push this boat off the shore and start sailing.

Lysa TerKeurst, thanks for your expert guidance along the way.

Tim Keller, your mentorship over many years has made me (Gabe) smarter, stronger, and more confident that, no matter what happens in the broader culture, our faith will last.

Our teams at Barna and Q work hard every day to educate Christians about what good faith can look like in the church and in every channel of culture. Thank you, Lance Villio (at Q) and Bill Denzel, Brooke Hempell, Roxanne Stone, and Todd White (at Barna) for leading our teams as we holed up to complete this project. Without your dedication, this book would never have come to life. Thanks to the team at Q: Christen Bohannon, Peter Court, Lauren Dillon, Annie Downs, Luke Dooley, Rob McCloskey, and Taylor McFerran. And to the team at Barna: Amy Brands, Joyce Chiu, Cory Maxwell-Coghlan, Inga Dahlstadt, Traci Hochmuth, Pam Jacob, Elaine Klautzch, and Brenda Usery. Thank you all for your commitment and hard work.

Other sincere thanks go to Brad Abare, George and Nancy Barna, Jeremy Blume, Eric Brown, Shari and Jeff Culver, David Denmark, Bill and Lorraine Frey, Steve Graves, Jim Henderson, Rick Ifland, Dale Kuehne, Matt and Kate Kinnaman, Britt Merrick, Lukas Naugle, Eddie and LaDonna Ramos, Larry Reichardt, Pete Richardson, Gareth and Andi Russell, Lauren Tomlin, and Jon Tyson.

To our parents, Gary and Marilyn Kinnaman and Melvin and Darlene Lyons: Thank you for pouring the truths of Scripture into us from our earliest years. That firm foundation continues to serve us well as we strive to serve the Lord.

Finally, to Rebekah, Jill, and our children—your generosity in giving us time and space to collaborate again means the world to us. You keep our families' faith alive even as we seek to help others. Thank you. We love you. Let's keep learning to practice good faith together.

NOTES

Chapter 1 Bad Faith, Good Faith

1. To be fair, American Christianity has its share of extremists (even if we are understandably reluctant to call the perpetrators "Christians"). From murdering abortion providers to hoisting "God Hates Fags" signs at funerals of US soldiers, these and other horrors are justifiably called acts of extremism.

2. Christopher Hitchens, *God Is Not Great: How Religion Poisons Everything* (New York: Twelve Books, 2009).

3. Unless otherwise noted, all statistics are from original research conducted by Barna Group.

4. Dallas Willard, *Knowing Christ Today* (New York: HarperOne, 2009).

5. Heart + Mind Strategies, "First Freedom," research sponsored by Maclellan Foundation, conducted among a representative sample of 2,507 US adults, August 2014.

6. Rob Cooper, "Forcing a Religion on Your Children Is as Bad as Child Abuse, Claims Atheist Professor Richard Dawkins," DailyMail.com, April 22, 2013, http://www.dailymail.co.uk/news/article-2312813/Richard-Dawkins-Forcing-religion-children-child-abuse-claims-atheist-professor.html.

7. Jeffrey Taylor, "David Brooks, Religious Clown: Debunking Phony Godsplaining from the New York Times' Laziest Column," Salon.com, March 15, 2015, http://www.salon.com/2015/03/15/david_brooks_religious_clown_debunking_phony_godsplaining_from_the_new_york_times_laziest_columnist/?utm_source=twitter&utm_medium=socialflow.

8. See especially Dale Kuehne, *Sex and the iWorld: Rethinking Relationship beyond an Age of Individualism* (Grand Rapids: Baker Academic, 2009).

9. See George Packer, *The Unwinding: An Inner History of the New America* (New York: Farrar, Straus and Giroux, 2013).

Chapter 2 Irrelevant

1. Heart + Mind Strategies, "First Freedom."
2. The Giving Institute, *Giving USA: The Annual Report on Philanthropy 2014* (Chicago: The Giving Institute, 2014), 106.
3. Ibid.
4. Barna OmniPoll, August 2015, *N* = 1,000.
5. David Brooks, *The Road to Character* (New York: Random House, 2015), 271.
6. The idea of "faithful presence" is explored in James Davison Hunter, *To Change the World* (New York: Oxford University Press, 2010). It's a concept that gives vision for the role Christians are to play when working in any industry—that is, to be a faithful presence.

Chapter 3 Extreme

1. Our sincere thanks to Pat MacMillan and Dee Alsop of Heart + Mind Strategies for their pioneering work to explore similar territory.

Chapter 4 The Tension We Feel and Why

1. For an in-depth examination, read Kirsten Powers, *The Silencing: How the Left Is Killing Free Speech* (Washington, DC: Regnery Publishing, 2015).
2. Mark Noll, "The Bible in American Public Life: 1860–2005," *Books & Culture*, July 2005, http://www.booksandculture.com/articles/2005/sepoct/15.07.html?paging=off.
3. Ibid.
4. See Gary Scott Smith, *Religion in the Oval Office: The Religious Lives of American Presidents* (New York: Oxford University Press, 2015).
5. See William R. Hutchison, *Religious Pluralism in America: The Contentious History of a Founding Ideal* (New Haven, CT: Yale University Press, 2003).
6. Our sincere thanks to Dale Kuehne for his work on the remaining moral rules. He should not be held responsible for any of our errors in logic or expression.
7. Torie Henderson, "I Believed the Propaganda," *Life Coaching for Parents*, May 29, 2012, http://lifecoachingforparents.com/i-believed-the-propaganda.
8. Dallas Willard, *Knowing Christ Today* (New York: HarperOne, 2009), 199–200.
9. To gain a much deeper understanding of how Epicureanism, the belief Lucretius was popularizing through his poem, has gained traction since the Enlightenment, see Stephen Greenblatt, PhD, *The Swerve: How the World Became Modern* (New York: W. W. Norton & Company, 2012).

Chapter 5 Love, Believe, Live

1. Chuck Colson and Nancy Pearcey, *How Now Shall We Live?* (Carol Stream, IL: Tyndale, 1999), 15.
2. Historian David Bebbington has offered a four-part definition that pretty well sums up what we mean when we call ourselves "evangelicals." *Conversionism* is the belief that lives need to be transformed through a "born-again" experience and a lifelong process of following Jesus. *Activism* is the expression and demonstration

of the gospel in missionary and social reform efforts. *Biblicism* is a high regard for and obedience to the Bible as Christians' ultimate authority. *Crucicentrism* is a stress on the sacrifice of Jesus Christ on the cross that makes possible the redemption of humanity. See David Bebbington, *Evangelicalism in Modern Britain: A History from the 1730s to the 1930s* (London: Unwin Hyman, 1989).

Chapter 6 The Right Questions

1. See David Kinnaman and Gabe Lyons, *unChristian: What a New Generation Really Thinks about Christianity . . . and Why It Matters* (Grand Rapids: Baker, 2007), especially chapter 8, "Judgmental," for an in-depth examination of this criticism.

2. Kirsten Powers, "Philadelphia Abortion Clinic Horror," *USA Today*, April 11, 2013, http://www.usatoday.com/story/opinion/2013/04/10/philadelphia-abortion -clinic-horror-column/2072577.

3. "What the News Isn't Telling You and Why We Can't Afford to Pretend It's Not Happening," *A Holy Experience*, http://www.aholyexperience.com/2015/05/into-iraq -2-what-the-news-isnt-telling-you-why-we-cant-afford-to-pretend-its-not-happen ing-sozans-impossible-choice-and-our-very-possible-one/.

4. http://www.preemptivelove.org.

5. Chuck Colson and Nancy Pearcey, *How Now Shall We Live?*

6. David Rowbotham, "Brisbane," Australian Poetry Library, http://www.poetry library.edu.au/poets/rowbotham-david/brisbane-0620083.

7. Tim Keller, "A New Kind of Urban Christian," *CityChurchYork*, February 28, 2012, http://www.citychurchyork.com/a-new-kind-of-urban-christian/.

8. http://darlingmagazine.org/mission.

9. Ibid.

10. Andy Crouch, *Culture Making: Recovering Our Creative Calling* (Downers Grove, IL: IVP, 2008).

Chapter 7 Who Will Lead?

1. Zach Ford, "Tracking Barack Obama's Position on Marriage Equality," *Think-Progress*, June 22, 2011, http://thinkprogress.org/lgbt/2011/06/22/250931/timeline -barack-obama-marriage-equality/.

2. Stephen V. Monsma, "Neither a Christian Nor a Secular Nation," *Capital Commentary*, July 20, 2015, http://www.capitalcommentary.com/principled-pluralism /neither-christian-nor-secular-nation.

3. Comedians in Cars Getting Coffee, http://comediansincarsgettingcoffee.com/ bill-maher-the-comedy-team-of-smug-and-arrogant.

4. President Bill Clinton made this remark on the one-hundredth anniversary of the *New Republic* publication. He also made it in a sit-down conversation with CNN's Anderson Cooper on national TV. See Conor Friedersdorf, "Bill Clinton on America's 'One Remaining Bigotry,'" *Atlantic*, November 21, 2014, http://www. theatlantic.com/politics/archive/2014/11/bill-clinton-americans-should-disagree -with-ideas-not-labels/383024/, the article reporting on his speech to the *New Republic* audience.

5. See Patricia Wen, "Catholic Charities Stuns State, Ends Adoptions," *Boston Globe*, March 11, 2006, http://www.boston.com/news/local/articles/2006/03/11/catholic_charities_stuns_state_ends_adoptions/.

6. Practice of faith inside a church building is a basic feature of most modern societies. What is unique about America is its protections of free exercise and association that engage our public square with faith. See Eleanor Albert, "Religion in China," Council on Foreign Relations, updated June 10, 2015, http://www.cfr.org/china/religion-china/p16272.

7. This is taken from James Madison's "Memorial and Remonstrance" papers of 1785. See http://press-pubs.uchicago.edu/founders/documents/amendI_religions43.html.

8. Senator Barack Obama, "Call to Renewal Keynote Address," June 28, 2006, http://obamaspeeches.com/081-Call-to-Renewal-Keynote-Address-Obama-Speech.htm.

9. Barack Obama worked for three years from June 1985 to May 1988 as director of the Developing Communities Project (DCP), a church-based community organization originally comprising eight Catholic parishes in Greater Roseland (Roseland, West Pullman, and Riverdale) on Chicago's far south side. See https://en.wikipedia.org/wiki/Early_life_and_career_of_Barack_Obama.

10. Os Guinness often asks this question when recognizing the unique gift America gives to the world in sorting through how religious liberty plays out. No other nation has quite figured this out, and America can be a shining light on this point. See Os Guinness, *A Free People's Suicide: Sustainable Freedom and the American Future* (Downers Grove, IL: IVP, 2012).

11. The following is the text Gabe summarizes from Charles Taylor, "The Meaning of Secularism" paper presented to the NYU Colloquium in Legal, Political, and Social Philosophy, New York, November 11, 2010:

> On one view (A), secularism is mainly concerned with controlling religion. Its task is to define the place of religion in public life, and to keep it firmly in this location. This doesn't need to involve strife or repression, provided various religious actors understand and respect these limits. But the various rules and measures which make up the secularist (or laïque) régime all have this basic purpose.
>
> On the other view (B), the main point of a secularist régime is to manage the religious and metaphysical-philosophical diversity of views (including non- and anti-religious views) fairly and democratically. Of course, this task will include setting certain limits to religiously motivated action in the public sphere, but it will also involve similar limits on those espousing non- or anti-religious philosophies. (For instance, the degree to which either can discriminate in certain relations, like hiring.) For B, religion is not the prime focus of secularism.
>
> The case I would like to make here is that B is much superior to A, at least for our time. The popularity of A is to be explained by certain Western histories of struggle in which secularist régimes came to be. But our present predicament is for the most part rather different than the one which generated these conflicts. It is above all, one of growing diversity in all Western democracies. For these reasons, B is more appropriate.

The full paper can be found at http://iasc-culture.org/THR/archives/Fall2010/ Taylor_lo.pdf.

12. John D. Inazu, *Confident Pluralism: Surviving and Thriving through Deep Difference* (Chicago: University of Chicago Press, 2016).

Chapter 8 Assimilate or Accommodate

1. Kathleen Parker, "Trigger Warnings, Colleges, and the 'Swaddled Generation,'" *Washington Post*, May 19, 2015, https://www.washingtonpost.com/opinions/the -swaddled-generation/2015/05/19/162ea17a-fe6a-11e4-805c-c3f407e5a9e9_story. html.

2. Greg Lukianoff and Jonathan Haidt, "The Coddling of the American Mind," *Atlantic*, September 2015, http://www.theatlantic.com/magazine/archive/2015/09/ the-coddling-of-the-american-mind/399356.

3. Ibid.

4. Ibid.

5. "Mike Bloomberg Delivers Remarks at Harvard University's 363rd Commencement Ceremony," *Mike Bloomberg*, May 29, 2014, http://www.mikebloomberg.com /news/mike-bloomberg-delivers-remarks-at-harvard-universitys-363rd-commence ment-ceremony.

6. See Les and Leslie Parrot, *The Good Fight* (Franklin, TN: Worthy Publishing, 2015).

Chapter 9 After the Revolution

1. Donna Freitas, *The End of Sex: How Hookup Culture Is Leaving a Generation Unhappy, Sexually Unfulfilled, and Confused about Intimacy* (New York: Basic Books, 2013).

2. Leigh Ann Wheeler, *How Sex Became a Civil Liberty* (London: Oxford University Press, 2012), 220.

3. "How Big Is the Pornography Industry in the United States?" *CovenantEyes*, June 1, 2012, http://www.covenanteyes.com/2012/06/01/how-big-is-the-pornography -industry-in-the-united-states/.

4. Ravi Somaiya, "Nudes Are Old News at Playboy," *New York Times*, October 12, 2015, http://www.nytimes.com/2015/10/13/business/media/nudes-are-old-news -at-playboy.html?_r=0.

5. Annalee Newitz, "Ashley Madison Code Shows More Women, and More Bots," *Gizmodo*, August 31, 2015, http://gizmodo.com/ashley-madison-code-shows-more -women-and-more-bots-1727613924.

6. Pamela Paul, *Pornified: How Pornography Is Damaging Our Lives, Our Relationships, and Our Families* (New York: St. Martin's Griffin, 2006).

7. "The Sexual Revolution's Coming Refugee Crisis," *Russell Moore*, July 7, 2015, https://www.russellmoore.com/2015/07/07/the-sexual-revolutions-coming-refugee -crisis/.

Chapter 10 Marriage, Family, and Friendships

1. "Children in Single Parent Families," Kids Count Data Center, http://datacenter. kidscount.org/data/tables/106-children-in-single-parent-families#detailed/1/any /false/36,868,867,133,38/any/429,430.

2. Eleanor Barkhorn, "Getting Married Late Is Great for College-Educated Women," *Atlantic*, March 15, 2013, http://www.theatlantic.com/sexes/archive/2013 /03/getting-married-later-is-great-for-college-educated-women/274040.

3. See David Kim and Barna Group, *20 and Something: Have the Time of Your Life (And Figure It All Out Too)* (Grand Rapids: Zondervan, 2014).

4. David P. Gushee and Christine C. Pohl, "Making Room: Recovering Hospitality as a Christian Tradition," *Christian Ethics Today* 33 (April 2001): 21, http://christian ethicstoday.com/cetart/index.cfm?fuseaction=Articles.main&ArtID=279.

5. Gregory Thompson, "Resurrection and the Household" (sermon, Trinity Presbyterian Church, Charlottesville, VA, May 17, 2015).

6. David P. Gushee and Christine C. Pohl, "Making Room."

Chapter 11 Life, Death, and Disability

1. See "The Epistle of Mathetes to Diognetus," second century, http://www.early christianwritings.com/text/diognetus-roberts.html.

2. Rodney Stark, *The Rise of Christianity* (San Francisco: HarperOne, 1997), 161.

3. Erin O'Neill, "Chris Smith Says More than 54 Million Abortions Have Been Performed since U.S. Supreme Court Decided *Roe v. Wade*," *PolitiFact*, March 18, 2012, http://www.politifact.com/new-jersey/statements/2012/mar/18/chris-smith /chris-smith-says-more-54-million-abortions-have-be.

4. The Planned Parenthood annual report for 2014 shows 327,000 abortions performed. That's roughly thirty-seven per hour or one every ninety seconds. Douglas Ernst, "Planned Parenthood Performed 327K Abortions in Fiscal 2014: 'We've Come a Long Way,'" *Washington Times*, January 1, 2015, http://www.washingtontimes.com /news/2015/jan/1/planned-parenthood-327k-abortions-fiscal-2014/. In contrast, they provided only 1,880 adoption referrals: D'Angelo Gore, "Planned Parenthood Services," FactCheck.org, September 4, 2015, http://www.factcheck.org /2015/09/planned-parenthoods-services/.

5. "Five Things You Need to Know about Adoption," Barna Group, November 15, 2013, https://www.barna.org/barna-update/family-kids/643-5-things-you-need-to -know-about-adoption; and Jedd Medefind, *Becoming Home: Adoption, Foster Care, and Mentoring: Living Out God's Heart for Orphans* (Grand Rapids: Zondervan, 2014).

6. Justin McCarthy, "Seven in Ten Americans Back Euthanasia," Gallup, June 18, 2014, http://www.gallup.com/poll/171704/seven-americans-back-euthanasia.aspx.

7. Brittany Maynard, "My Right to Death with Dignity at 29," CNN, November 2, 2014, http://www.cnn.com/2014/10/07/opinion/maynard-assisted-suicide-cancer -dignity/.

8. https://www.youtube.com/watch?v=1lHXH0Zb2QI.

9. "Brittany Maynard, the Terminally Ill Woman Choosing to Die Nov 1 Tells CNN: Now 'Doesn't Seem like the Right Time,'" WGNTV.com, October 30, 2014, http://wgntv.com/2014/10/29/brittany-maynard-the-terminially-ill-woman-chosing -to-die-nov-1-tells-cnn-now-doesnt-seem-like-the-right-time/.

10. Kim Kuo, "Assisted Suicide and Real Death with Dignity," *Christianity Today*, September 15, 2015, http://www.christianitytoday.com/ct/2015/september/assisted-suicide-and-real-death-with-dignity.html.

11. "Episode 23: Pro-life, Pro-choice," *The Liturgists*, September 18, 2015, http://www.theliturgists.com/podcast/2015/9/6/episode-23-pro-life-pro-choice.

Chapter 12 Race and Prejudice

1. I found out later that, no, the Tennessee Residence was never a plantation. It was built in 1929, sixty-six years after the Emancipation Proclamation. But that morning I had no idea.

2. From this convening we created a podcast that gives even more context and voice to the depth of this conversation on race. Listen to the entire forty-five-minute podcast here: http://qideas.org/articles/q-roundtable-podcast-race/.

3. Eight out of ten evangelicals are white, compared to less than 65 percent of the general population (Barna *Cities and States* Database, 2009–15). N=30,065.

4. Lisa Sharon Harper's argument is confirmed by the research of Michael Emerson in *Divided by Faith: Evangelical Religion and the Problem of Race in America* (New York: Oxford University Press, 2001).

5. You can view the entire eighteen-minute Q Talk interview at http://qideas.org/videos/lessons-from-ferguson-boston.

Chapter 13 The Gay Conversation

1. Gary J. Gates and Frank Newport, "Special Report: 3.4% of U.S. Adults Identify as LGBT," Gallup, October 18, 2012, http://www.gallup.com/poll/158066/special-report-adults-identify-lgbt.aspx.

2. The Q podcast provides a five-episode series that delves deeply into the sexuality conversation, including twenty-five voices who weigh in on the conversation. To hear from people who can provide insights, from personal experience, on how we can engage this conversation with a loving posture, listen at www.qideas.org/podcast.

3. Writers such as Matthew Vines, David Gushee, Tony Campolo, and many others have used a similar line of thinking over the past few years to justify their affirmation of same-sex marriage within the church.

4. Boston's Tremont Temple, chartered in 1839, set out this clear standard at the founding of their church. See their history page at http://tremonttemple.org/about/our-story/.

5. For many more examples of Christians on the right side of history, see Kevin DeYoung, *What Does the Bible Really Teach about Homosexuality?* (Wheaton, IL: Crossway, 2015).

6. For a deeper reading on this passage, see John Piper, "How Paul Worked to Overcome Slavery," *DesiringGod*, September 3, 2009, http://www.desiringgod.org/articles/how-paul-worked-to-overcome-slavery.

7. Thomas D. Williams, "Poll: Support for Gay Marriage Has Fallen after Obergefell," *Breitbart*, July 19, 2015, http://www.breitbart.com/big-government/2015/07/19/poll-support-for-gay-marriage-has-fallen-after-obergefell.

8. Mainline Protestant denominations include American Baptist Churches in the USA, the Episcopal Church, the Evangelical Lutheran Church in America, the Presbyterian Church (USA), the United Church of Christ, and the United Methodist Church.

Chapter 14 We Can't Live without Intimacy

1. Julie Rodgers, who identifies as a gay Christian, makes this statement in her Q Talk at Q Women on November 13, 2014, http://qideas.org/videos/freedom-through-constraint/.

2. See my entire conversation with Gene Robinson at Stanford's Memorial Church at https://youtu.be/l4avq4Bk9c8.

3. American Psychological Association, "Answers to Your Questions," www.apa.org/topics/lgbt/orientation.pdf.

> There is no consensus among scientists about the exact reasons that an individual develops a heterosexual, bisexual, gay, or lesbian orientation. Although much research has examined the possible genetic, hormonal, developmental, social, and cultural influences on sexual orientation, no findings have emerged that permit scientists to conclude that sexual orientation is determined by any particular factor or factors. Many think that nature and nurture both play complex roles; most people experience little or no sense of choice about their sexual orientation.

4. In my public conversations with both Andrew Sullivan and Eugene Robinson, they both acknowledged that orientation is formed after the age of three.

5. Jenel Williams Paris, *The End of Sexual Identity: Why Sex Is Too Important to Define Who We Are* (Downers Grove, IL: IVP, 2011) is a great read that unpacks how fluid our sexuality is and provides a very helpful continuum from "The Kinsey Scale" on page 45.

6. Stanton L. Jones and Mark A. Yarhouse, *Ex-Gays?: A Longitudinal Study of Religiously Mediated Change in Sexual Orientation* (Downers Grove, IL: IVP Academic, 2009). See also http://www.sexualidentityinstitute.org/resources/faq.

7. "Support for Same-Sex Marriage at Record High, but Key Segments Remain Opposed," Pew Research Center, June 8, 2015, http://www.people-press.org/2015/06/08/support-for-same-sex-marriage-at-record-high-but-key-segments-remain-opposed.

8. Charles Taylor, *The Ethics of Authenticity* (Cambridge: Harvard University Press, 1992), 142.

9. Ibid.

10. Ibid.

11. Read more about how feelings don't always point to reality in David and Jason Benham, "The One Thing Bruce Jenner Really Needs," *WND*, June 14, 2015, http://www.wnd.com/2015/06/the-1-thing-bruce-jenner-really-needs/.

12. "Caitlyn Jenner Is Finally 'Free' on *Vanity Fair*'s Cover," Vanity Fair Video, June 1, 2015, http://video.vanityfair.com/watch/vanity-fair-cover-caitlyn-jenner-is-finally-free.

13. C. S. Lewis, *First and Second Things* (London: Fount, 1985), 22.

14. Tim Keller, "The Bible and Same-Sex Relationships: A Review Article," *Redeemer Report*, June 2015, http://www.redeemer.com/redeemer-report/article/the _bible_and_same_sex_relationships_a_review_article.

15. This is, in fact, the title of his book on the subject.

16. Matt. 16:24–25; cf. Luke 9:23–24.

17. Dayna Olson-Getty, "The Witness of Celibate Sexuality: A Challenge to Evangelical Theology and Practice of Single Sexuality" (unpublished paper, Inter-Varsity Ministry Exchange), 10.

18. Eve Tushnet, *Gay and Catholic: Accepting My Sexuality, Finding Community, Living My Faith* (Notre Dame, IN: Ave Maria Press, 2014), 126.

19. Matthew Jones, "Hospitality," *Gay Subtlety*, August 9, 2012, https://gaysubtlety. wordpress.com/2012/08/09/hospitality.

20. Tushnet's book, along with Wesley Hill, *Washed and Waiting: Reflections on Christian Faithfulness and Homosexuality* (Grand Rapids: Zondervan, 2010) and Wesley Hill, *Spiritual Friendship: Finding Love in the Church as a Gay Celibate Christian* (Grand Rapids: Brazos Press, 2015), are great guides for walking alongside gay Christians as members of their spiritual family.

21. Tushnet, *Gay and Catholic*, 207.

Chapter 15 Five Ways to Be Faithful

1. Kirsten Powers, "Jim Crow Laws for Gays and Lesbians?" *USA Today*, February 19, 2014, http://www.usatoday.com/story/opinion/2014/02/18/gays-lesbians-kansas -bill-religious-freedom-christians-column/5588643.

2. From an interview conducted by Preston Sprinkle on September 23, 2015, for the Q Podcast. Used with permission from Christopher Yuan.

3. Preston Sprinkle, *People to Be Loved: Why Homosexuality Is Not Just an Issue* (Grand Rapids: Zondervan, 2015), 35.

4. Ibid., 36.

5. From an interview conducted by Gabe Lyons on September 28, 2015, for the Q Podcast. Used with permission from Dean Curry.

6. These are lessons I've learned from reading James K. A. Smith, *Desiring the Kingdom: Worship, Worldview, and Cultural Formation* (Grand Rapids: Baker Academic, 2009) and James K. A. Smith, *Imagining the Kingdom: How Worship Works* (Grand Rapids: Baker Academic, 2013).

7. James K. A. Smith's work and writings (see above) have had a profound influence on our thinking about the relationship between the church and state.

8. Gabe's book *The Next Christians* was first subtitled in 2010 *The Good News about the End of Christian America*. In the first three chapters, he makes the case that great positives can come from the changing landscape of America.

Chapter 16 Firm Center, Soft Edges

1. Dallas Willard, *Knowing Christ Today*.

2. Barry Corey, *Love Kindness: Discover the Power of a Forgotten Christian Virtue* (Carol Stream, IL: Tyndale, 2016).

Chapter 17 Church in a New World

1. Andrew Liddle, "Faith in Scotland Offers Hope to Christian Groups," *Courier Dundee*, September 2, 2015, 17.

2. David O'Reilly, "A Study Asks: What's a Church's Economic Worth?" *Philadelphia Inquirer*, February 1, 2011, http://articles.philly.com/2011-02-01/news/27 092987_1_partners-for-sacred-places-congregations-churches. See also "Letters: Church's 'Negative' Score Result of 'Counting Error,'" *Philadelphia Inquirer*, February 7, 2011, http://articles.philly.com/2011-02-07/news/27105556_1_partners-for -sacred-places-housing-values-congregation.

3. "World Vision: Church Communities Australia Report," research conducted by McCrindle, November 2015–January 2015. See infographic at http://www.mccrindle. com.au/resources/World-Vision-Church-and-Community-Infographic_Digital. pdf.

4. Monica Lara, "Mission Church Hosts Prom for Some Special Guests," *Ventura County Star*, May 8, 2012, http://www.vcstar.com/news/mission-church-hosts-prom -for-some-special.

5. Barna Group, *The State of Discipleship: A Barna Report Produced in Partnership with The Navigators* (Ventura, CA: Barna Group, 2015).

6. Willard, *Knowing Christ Today*, page 198. This entire chapter is worth the price of admission to the book, especially his discussion of the importance of religious belief as *knowledge*, not merely beliefs or commitment. We highly recommend it to pastors and other church leaders.

7. "The State of Spiritual Leadership" is a two-year study Barna conducted in 2014 and 2015 on behalf of Pepperdine University to assess pastors' perceptions of their physical, emotional, spiritual, and mental health; pastors' perceptions of their congregation's overall health; and US adults' perceptions of Christian ministers.

8. Rod Dreher, "'Resident Aliens' and the Benedict Option," *American Conservative*, September 1, 2015, http://www.theamericanconservative.com/dreher/resident -aliens-the-benedict-option.

9. Augustine, *The City of God* (excerpts on the Two Cities), Fordham University Medieval Sourcebook, http://legacy.fordham.edu/halsall/source/aug-city2.asp.

10. Robert Louis Wilken, "The Church as Culture," *First Things*, April 2004, http://www.firstthings.com/article/2004/04/the-church-as-culture.

11. For more detailed treatment on managing technology and practicing Sabbath as expressions of a countercultural life, see chapter 8 of Gabe's book *The Next Christians*.

Chapter 18 Faithful in Exile

1. Max DePree, *Leadership Is an Art* (New York: Doubleday Business, 1989).

2. Todd Starnes, "Houston Mayor Drops Bid to Subpoena Pastors' Sermons," *Fox News Opinion*, October 29, 2014, http://www.foxnews.com/opinion/2014/10/29 /houston-mayor-drops-bid-to-subpoena-pastors-sermons.html.

3. David French, "Gordon College Keeps Its Faith and Its Accreditation," *National Review*, May 1, 2015, http://www.nationalreview.com/article/417788/gordon-college -keeps-its-faith-and-its-accreditation-david-french.

GLOSSARY

Generations

A "generation" is an analytical tool for understanding culture and the people within it. It is based on the idea that people born during a certain period of time are influenced by a unique set of circumstances; global events; moral and social values; technologies; and cultural and behavioral norms. We use the following generations:

Millennials: born between 1984 and 2002

Gen-Xers: born between 1965 and 1983

Boomers: born between 1946 and 1964

Elders: born 1945 and earlier

Faith Segments

To understand people better, Barna groups them into various categories based on their religious beliefs and faith practices. We use the following faith segments:

Self-identified Christians: people who select "Christian" from a list of religious affiliations

Other faith: people who select a faith other than Christianity from a list of religious affiliations

No faith: people who select "atheist," "agnostic," or "none" from a list of religious affiliations

Practicing Christians: self-identified Christians who say their faith is very important in their lives and have attended a worship service within the past month; this group includes practicing Protestants (including mainline and non-mainline adherents) and practicing Catholics

Evangelicals: self-identified Christians who have made a commitment to Jesus Christ that is still important in their lives today and believe that, when they die, they will go to heaven because they have confessed their sins and accepted Jesus as their Savior. They also meet seven additional criteria:

1. They say faith is very important in their lives.
2. They believe they have a personal responsibility to share their belief in Christ with non-Christians.
3. They believe Satan exists.
4. They believe eternal salvation is possible only through grace, not works.
5. They believe Jesus Christ lived a sinless life.
6. They believe the Bible is accurate in all it teaches.
7. They describe God as the all-knowing, all-powerful, perfect deity who created the universe and still rules it today.

Classification as an evangelical does not depend on church attendance or denominational affiliation, and respondents are not asked to describe themselves as "evangelical."

According to the definitions shown above, evangelicals represent just fewer than 19 million US adults, and practicing Christians comprise about 72 million. There is some overlap between the two groups: 95 percent of evangelicals are practicing Christians and 21 percent of practicing Christians are evangelicals.

ABOUT THE RESEARCH

Throughout this book we refer to primary research that is not footnoted. These statistics and data-based analyses are derived from a series of national public-opinion surveys conducted by Barna Group.

Dates		Collection method	Sample size	Sampling error*
2009–2015	Barna's *Cities & States* database / US adults	telephone and online	30,535	±0.5
November 2012	US adults	telephone	1,008	±2.9
July 2014	Christian clergy	telephone and online	1,449 (1,286 Protestant; 163 Catholic)	±2.4
July 2014	Clergy from other faith traditions	telephone and online	159	±7.7
January 8–February 11, 2015	US adults	telephone and online	2,010	±2.0
April 29–May 1, 2015	US adults	online	1,025	±2.9
June 27–28, 2015	US adults	telephone	1,012	±2.9
July 3–9, 2015	US adults	online	1,237	±2.6
August 17–21, 2015	US adults	online	1,000	±3.0
August 24–26, 2015	US adults	online	1,000	±3.0

*Percentage points; sampling error reflects a 95-percent confidence level.

All of the research studies identified above, with the exception of the faith-leader research, were independently funded by Barna Group. The clergy research was conducted on behalf of the Maclellan Foundation.

Once data was collected, minimal statistical weights were applied to several demographic variables to more closely correspond to known national averages. On questions for which tracking was available, findings from these recent studies were compared to Barna's database of national studies from the past three decades. Data from the clergy study were minimally weighted on denomination and region to more closely reflect the demographic characteristics of churches in each media market.

When researchers describe the accuracy of survey results, they usually provide the estimated amount of "sampling error." This refers to the degree of possible inaccuracy that could be attributed to interviewing a group of people that is not completely representative of the population from which they were drawn. For the general population surveys, see the table above for maximum sampling error.

There is a range of other errors that can influence survey results (e.g., biased question wording, question sequencing, inaccurate recording of responses, inaccurate data tabulation, etc.)—errors whose influence on the findings cannot be statistically estimated. Barna makes every effort to overcome these possible errors at every stage of research.

ABOUT THE AUTHORS

David Kinnaman is author of *unChristian* and *You Lost Me*. He is president of Barna Group, a leading research and communications company. He has supervised or directed interviews with nearly one million individuals and overseen hundreds of nationwide research studies since 1995. Barna's body of research is frequently quoted by church leaders and in major media outlets. Kinnaman speaks on topics including cultural and spiritual trends, teenagers and young adults, leadership, and vocation and calling. He and his wife, Jill, live in California with their three children.

Gabe Lyons is author of *unChristian* and *The Next Christians*. He is the founder of Q, a learning community that educates and mobilizes Christians to think well and advance good in society. Called "sophisticated and orthodox" by *The New York Times*, Q represents the perspective of a new generation of Christians. Gabe speaks on cultural issues where faith intersects public life. He lives in Nashville with his wife, Rebekah, and their three children.

Barna

KNOWLEDGE TO NAVIGATE A CHANGING WORLD

If you're like most Christians and church leaders, you're wrestling with how to navigate a complex and changing culture. You need a trusted advisor, someone who can help you figure out what's happening and the next steps to take.

Barna can provide you with relevant, data-driven insights on today's society. For more than 30 years, Barna has conducted over one million interviews through the course of thousands of studies and has become a go-to source for insights about faith, culture, leadership, and generations.

Visit Barna.org

- •Sign up for Barna's free research releases and newsletters
- •Discover the latest Barna research and resources
- •Find out more about custom research for your organization

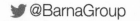 @BarnaGroup    facebook.com/BarnaGroup/

Stay Curious. Think Well. Advance Good.

Continue your learning by watching our top ten Q Talks
curated to help you live good faith.

WWW.QIDEAS.ORG/GF

Join the conversation that educates and empowers
Christians to advance the common good in your city.

WWW.QCOMMONS.COM

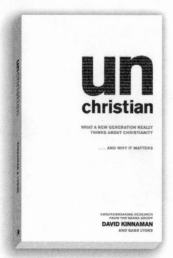